13435 N.E. Whitaker Way - Portland, Or. 97230
PH(503)254-9100 Fax (503)252-9508

DEDICATION PAGE

We have a new blessing in our family. Jake and Abby have been joined by a little brother, Nicholas Dane. Grandma hasn't met yet, but will be soon. Jacob says "Oh Grandma he's so cute." Abby politely informed me in her curt little way that "he really wanted to play with her, but he kept falling asleep, and she just didn't know why." At nationals this week someone said how are your boys, I feel like even though I've never met them I've grown up with them. They are wonderful and truly are my greatest Blessings in life.

This book also goes to Bob and Fleeta Jennings of D.C.& C. for all the wonderful pieces they supplied and all of their staff for tolerating my running in and out and of course, wanting this or that immediately.

Never fail to Count Your Blessings big or small. Nick is a tiny blessing at this time whom I'm sure will grow up to be a big blessing.

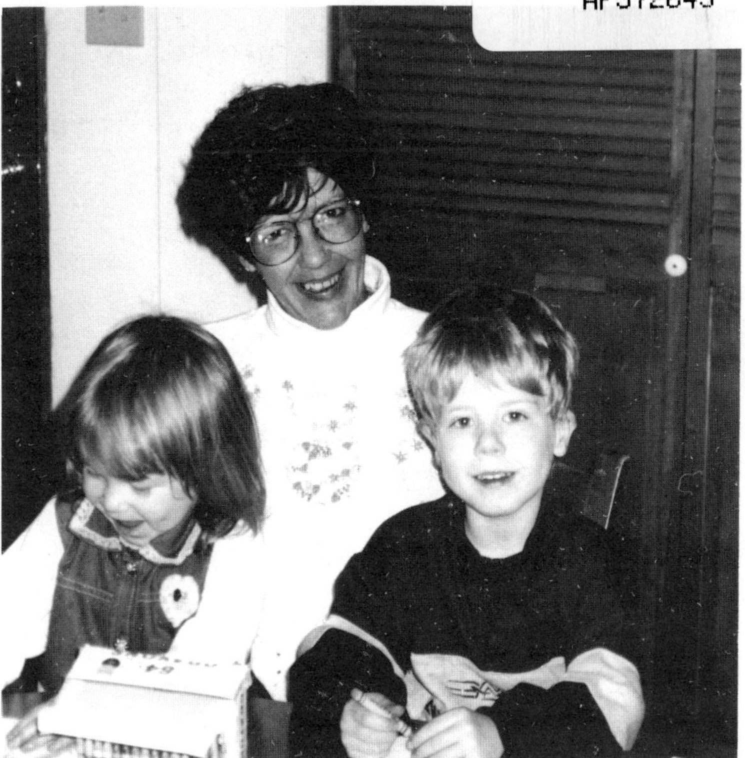

COUNT YOUR BLESSINGS

LOVE MAKES THE BEST MEMORIES

Supplies:

DecoArt Americana Colors:

DA67 Black
DA1 White
DA60 Mocha
DA65 Dk. Chocolate
DA97 Rookwood Red
DA133 Hauser Dark Green
DA164 Lt. Buttermilk
DA168 Golden Straw
DA6 Pineapple
DA109 Taupe
DA149 Silver Sage Green
DA96 Red Iron Oxide
DA57 Jade Green
DA162 Antique Mauve
DA49 Dark Pine
DA3 Buttermilk
DA194 Marigold
DA107 Teal Green
DA26 Mauve
DA157 Black Green
DA8 Yellow Ochre
DA196 Tangelo Orange
DA173 Khaki Tan
DA27 Gooseberry Pink
DA50 Forest Green
DA7 Moon Yellow
DA185 Light French Blue
DA23 Peaches N Cream
DA141 Blue Violet
DA52 Avocado
DA184 French Vanilla
DA186 French Mauve
DA7 Moon Yellow
DA18 Country Red
DA43 Salem Blue
DA153 Egg Shell
DA158 Antique Teal
DA94 Mississippi Mud
DA82 Evergreen
DA166 Deep Midnight Blue
DA195 Light French Blue
DA163 Honey Brown
DA58 Antique White
DA150 Royal Purple
DA41 Country Blue
DA106 Lt. Avocado
DA156 Antique Rose
DA71 Glorious Gold
DA86 Uniform Blue
DA189 Summer Lilac
DA168 Golden Straw
DA160AntiqueMaroon
Da62 Terra-Cotta
DA100 Ultra Deep Blue
DA112 Cranberry Wine
DA111 Grey Sky

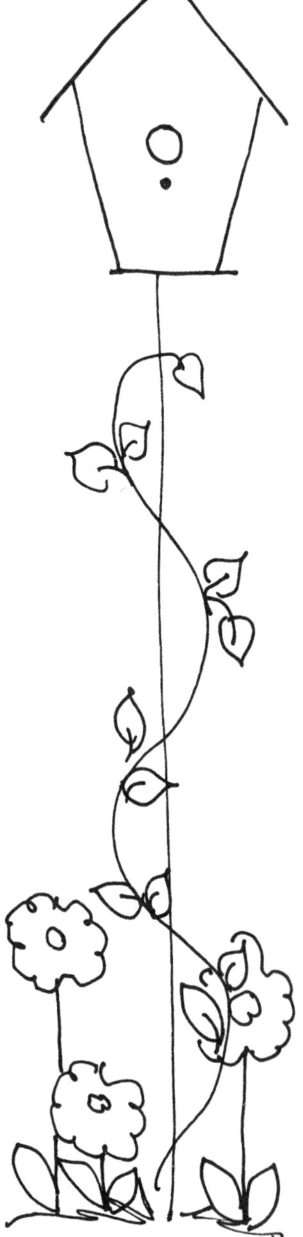

DecoArt Royal Metallics:

DM03 Royal Gold
DM01 Pale Gold

DecoArt Patio Paint:

DCP18 Woodland Brown
DCP21 Wrought Iron Black
DCP16 Patio Brick
DCP10 Summer Sky Blue

DecoArt Specialty Products:

DS17 Multi Purpose Sealer
Glaze Medium
DAS13 Matte Spray
DAS9 Snow Tex
DS18 Faux
DAS8 Weathered Wood

Brushes:

Loew-Cornell

La-Corneille Golden

Series No.7050 Script Liner Nos. 1 and 3
Series No. 7550 Wash 1/2", 3/4", and 1"
Series No. 7300 Square Shader Nos. 4, 6, 8, 10, and 12
Series No. 7520 Filbert Rake Nos. 1/4" and 1/2"

Suppliers:

D.C.&C.
428 S. Zelta
Wichita, Ks. 67207
Fax 316-685-7606
1-800-835-3013

TWIG BARN BIRDHOUSE

DecoArt Americana Colors:

DA67 Black
DA6 Pineapple
DA41 Country Blue
DA1 White

DecoArt Patio Paint:

DCP18 Woodland Brown
DCP16 Patio Brick
DCP21 Wrought Iron Black
DCP24 Clear Coat

DecoArt Specialty Products:

DS18 Multi Purpose
DAS13 Matte Spray

Surface by DC&C

Twig Barn Birdhouse #368212
Tin-tiques: 1 Folk Art Hearts #24-7203 and 1 #24-7204
Bird #24-7128
Raffia #36-0364

HOME
TWEET
HOME

Miscellaneous Supplies:

Plaid Paper Wired Ribbon
Hot Glue Gun

Painting Instructions:

1. Apply one even coat of **Multi Purpose Sealer** to all tin pieces.
2. Apply one even coat of **Clear Coat** to terra-cotta roof.
3. Float the stomach of the bird with **Black.** Float his back and head with **Country Blue** plus a touch of **White.** Float one heart with **Pineapple** and one with **Country Blue.** Dot the bird and the yellow heart with **Country Blue**, dot blue with **Pineapple.**
4. Liner-work **Black.**
5. Antique the wall section with **Patio Brick.**
6. Antique the roof **Woodland Brown** plus a touch of **Wrought Iron Black.**

To Finish:

Glue bow and raffia into place and then tin pieces.

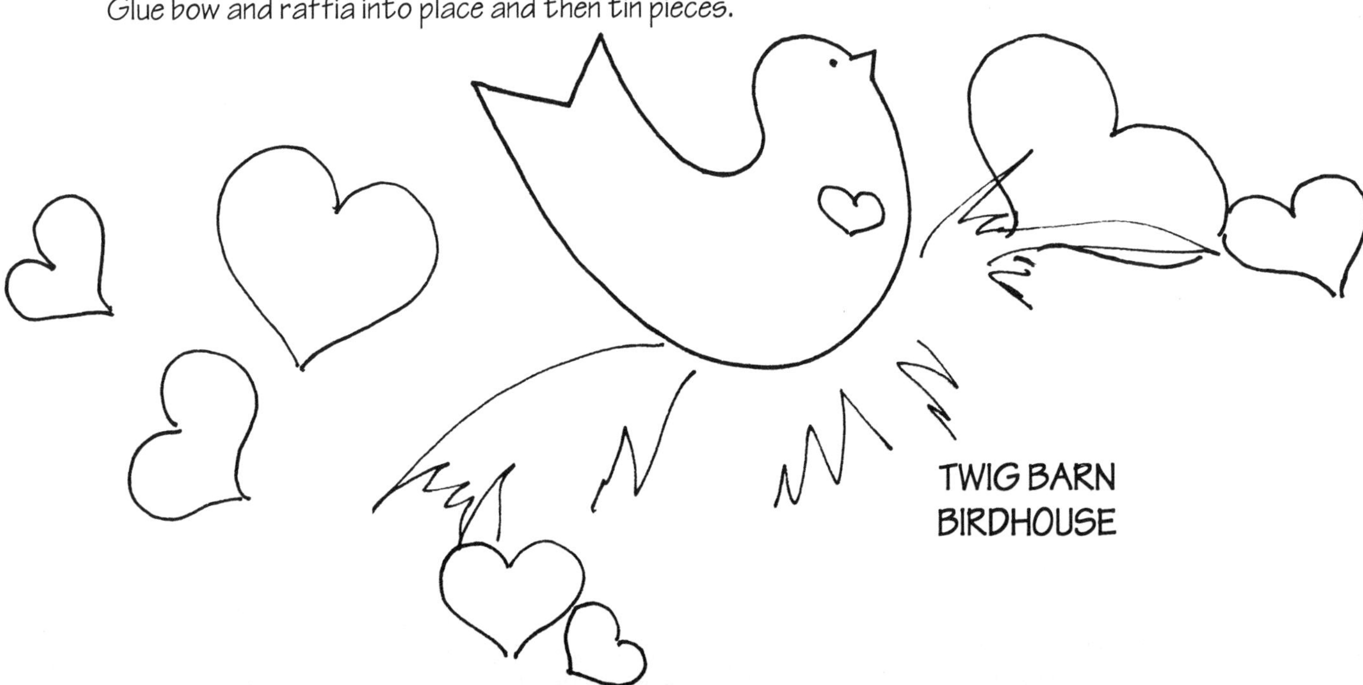

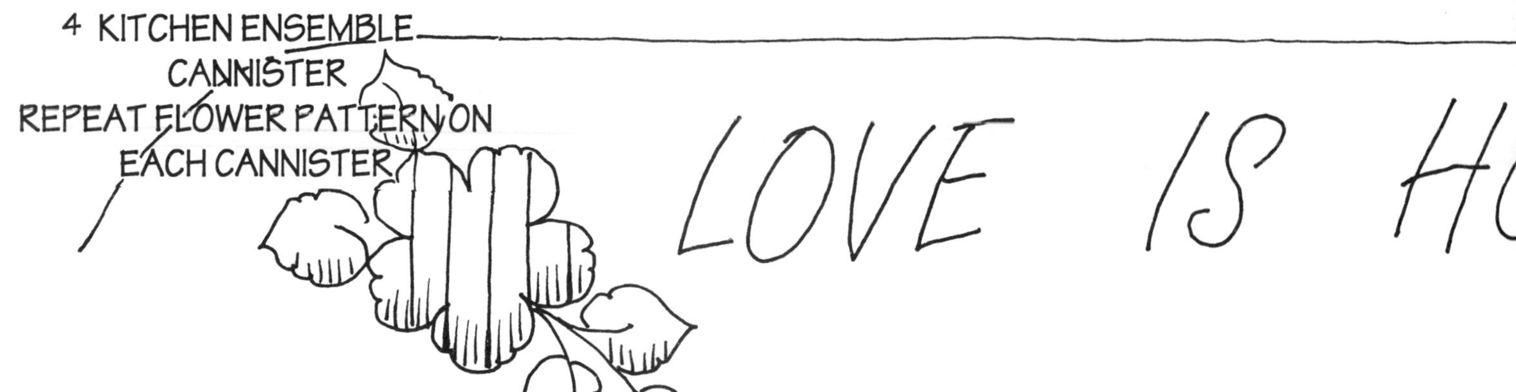

KITCHEN ENSEMBLE

DecoArt Americana Acrylics:

DA86 Uniform Blue
DA1 White
DA50 Forest Green
DA18 Country Red
DA67 Black
DA27 Gooseberry Pink
DA128 Deep Burgundy
DA168 Golden Straw

DecoArt Patio Paint:

DCP18 Woodland Brown

DecoArt Specialty Products:

DS18 Multi Purpose Sealer
DAS13 Matte Spray

SUGAR

Surfaces by DC&C

Shelf with Three Canisters #28-4010
Matchstick Holder #28-4011
Rusty Tin Birdhouse Silhouette #24-7341
Rusty Tin Basket #24-7400
Candle Holder #29-5178
Candle Lamp Shade Holder #29-5152
Rusty Tin Lamp Shade #29-5166

FLOUR

TEA

Miscellaneous Supplies:

Bond 527 Glue
Red, Yellow, and Blue Buttons
Fabric

Apply one even coat of Multi Purpose Sealer to all tin pieces.

Painting Instructions for Basket:

Basecoat chickens in **White.** Basecoat comb and waddle in **Country Red**. Beaks **Golden Straw.**

Painting Instructions Lamp:

Basecoat the stand, lamp shade holder and ring around shade in **Uniform Blue.** On shade do band in **Deep Burgundy** and **Black.** Basecoat chickens in **White.** Basecoat comb and waddle in **Country Red.** Beaks **Golden Straw.**

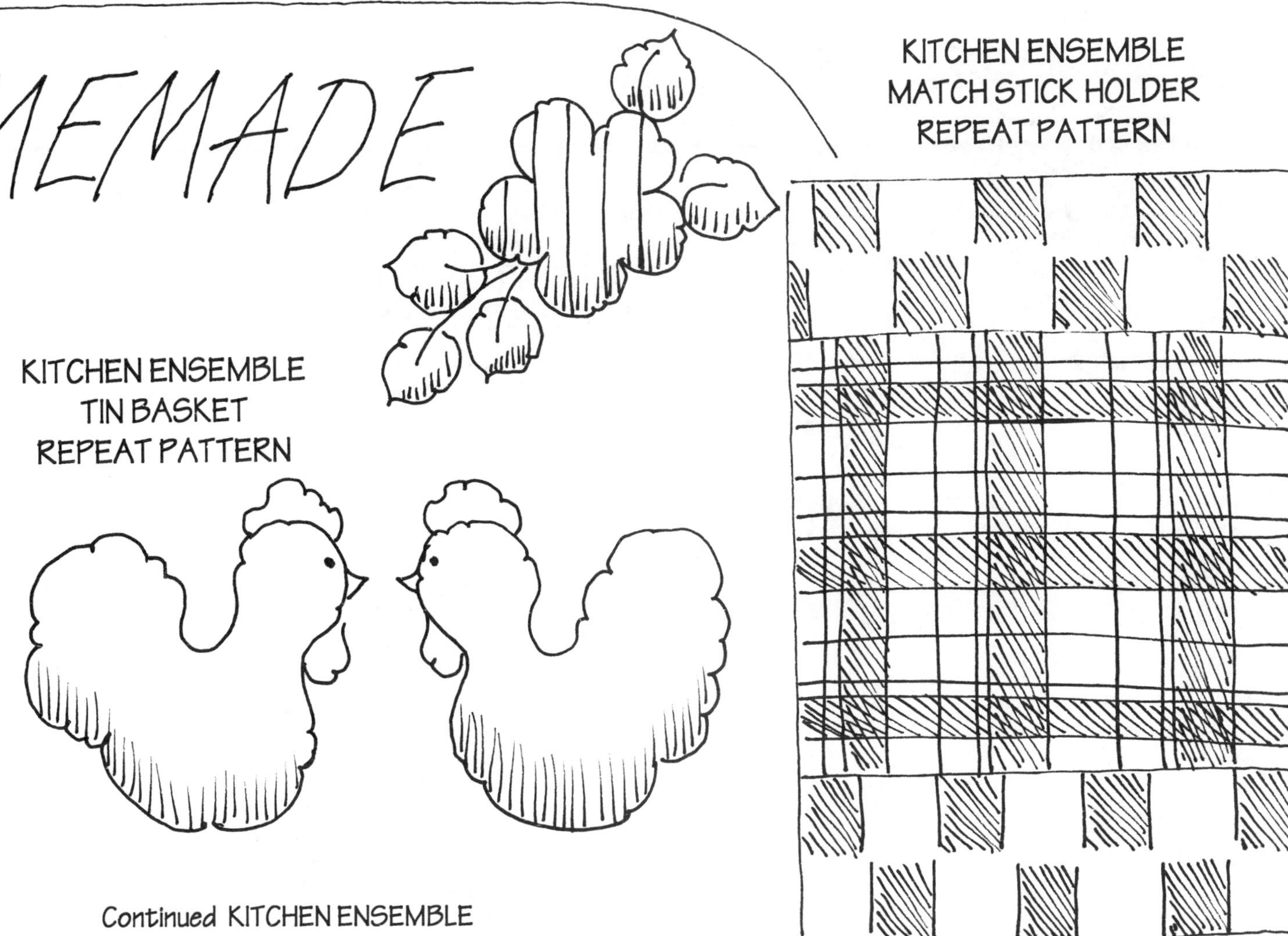

Continued KITCHEN ENSEMBLE

Painting Instructions for Matchholder:

Basecoat in **Deep Burgundy** and **Uniform Blue.** To do the plaid on the blue areas do all horizontal and then all vertical. Using **Gooseberry Pink. Golden Straw,** and **White.** Do checks on burgundy in **White.** Do all banding in **Black.**

Painting Instructions for Canisters and Tin Birdhouse Silhouette:

1. On canisters basecoat the **Uniform Blue, Deep Burgundy** and **White** areas.
2. On birdhouse basecoat chicken in **White.** Basecoat comb and waddle in **Country Red.** Beaks **Golden Straw.**
3. Basecoat flowers in **Gooseberry Pink,** stripe with **Golden Straw** and **Uniform Blue.**
4. Stroke leaves with a double-load of **Forest Green** and **Golden Straw.**
5. Do lettering on canisters in **Uniform Blue** and on shelf in **Uniform Blue** plus a touch of **White.**

To Finish all Pieces:

1. Do liner-work in **Black.**
2. With Bond 527 Glue on buttons.
3. Spatter with **Black.** Apply an even coat of **Matte Spray.** Antique with **Woodland Brown.**
4. Glue ties and bows in place.

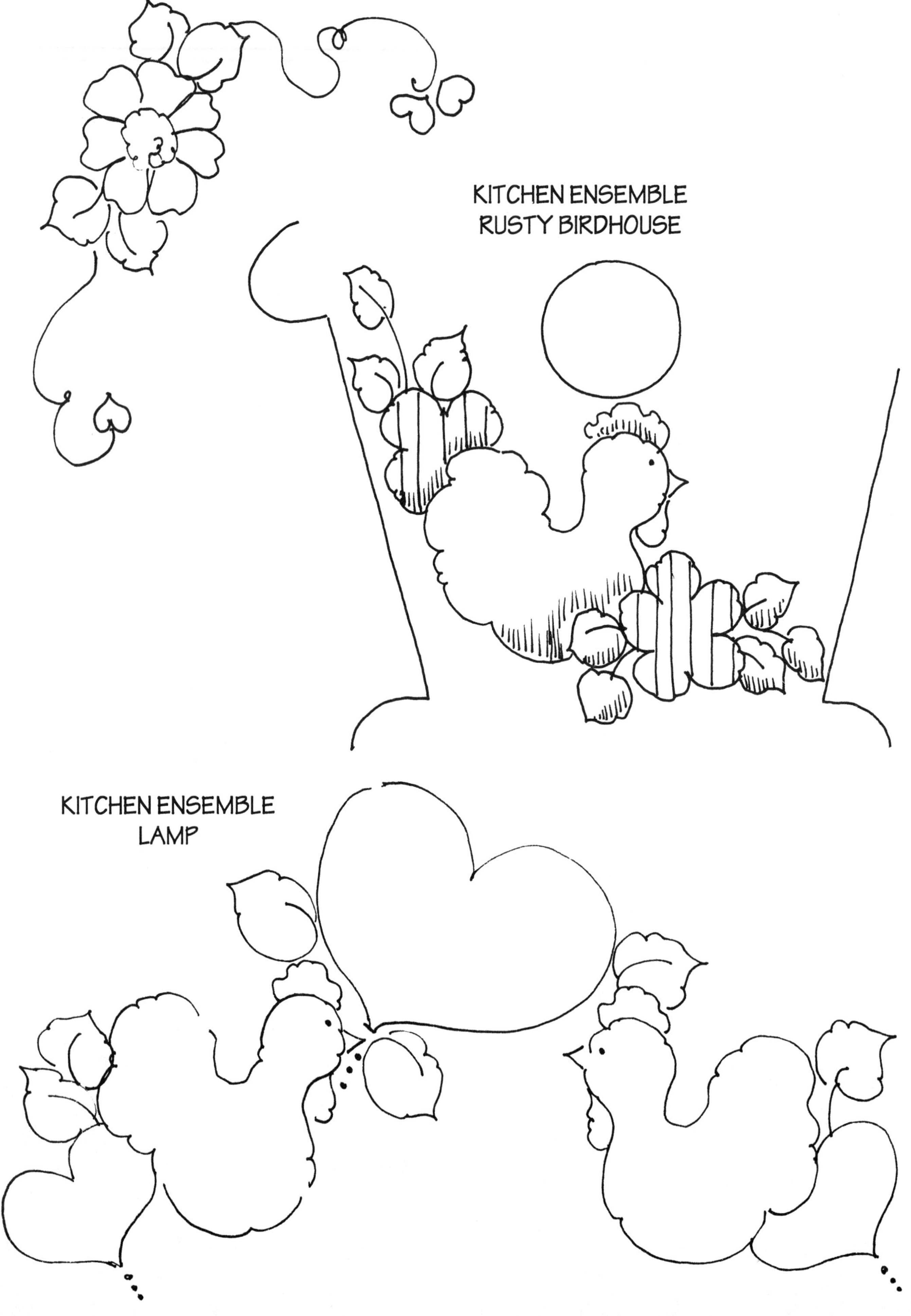
KITCHEN ENSEMBLE
RUSTY BIRDHOUSE
KITCHEN ENSEMBLE
LAMP

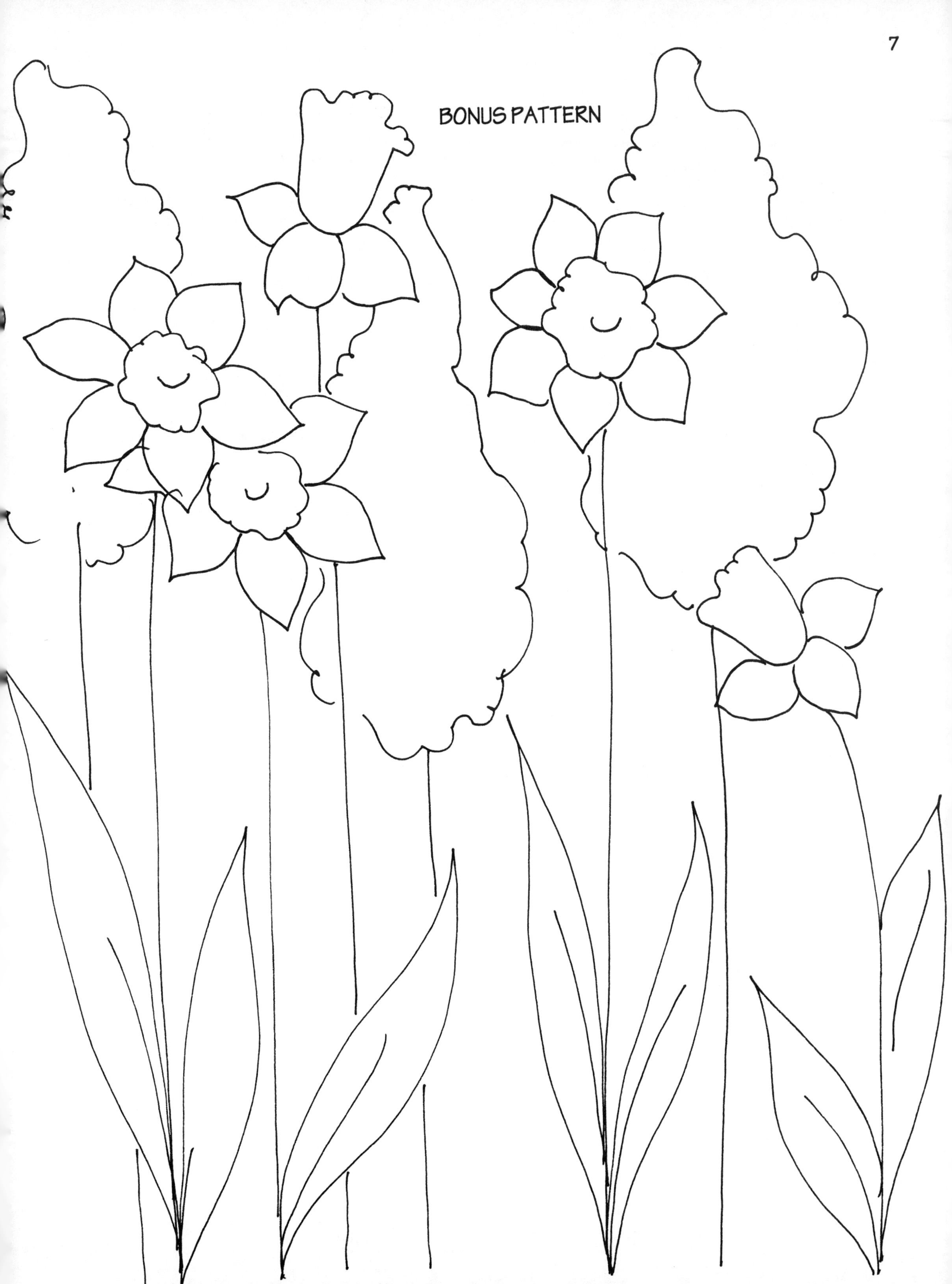
BONUS PATTERN

FLOWER POT BIRDHOUSE

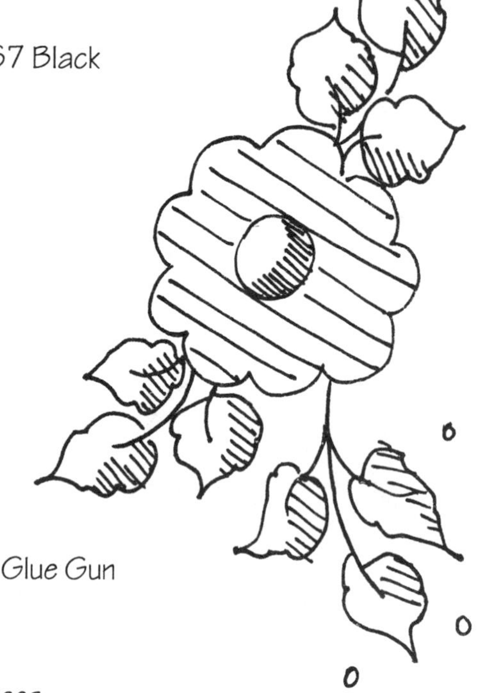

DecoArt Americana Colors:

DA86 Uniform Blue | DA1 White | DA67 Black
DA168 Golden Straw | DA96 Red Iron Oxide

DecoArt Patio Paint:

DCP18 Woodland Brown

DecoArt Specialty Products:

DS18 Multi Purpose | DAS13 Matte Spray

Surface by DC&C

Flower Pot Birdhouse #28-0176
Tin-tiques:
Stars - Three of each #24-7222 and #24-7223
Raffia #36-0364

Miscellaneous Supplies:

Old Brush for Stippling | Tacky Glue | Hot Glue Gun

Painting Instructions:

1. Apply one even coat of **Multi Purpose Sealer** to all tin pieces.
2. Basecoat the bottom part of the pot in **Red Iron Oxide.** Basecoat the upper in **Uniform Blue.**
3. To do the plaid in the center section of the red, do all vertical stripes and then all of the horizontal stripes. Do the **White**, then **Golden Straw** and then **Black.**
4. Do the next section **Golden Straw** dots, then bottom section **Uniform Blue** crosshatching.
5. Stipple the outside edge of the stars in **Golden Straw.**
6. Glue stars in place.
7. Spatter with **Black**. Spary with **Matte Spray**. Antique with **Woodland Brown.**

To Finish:

Glue large raffia bow in place.

FLOWER POT BIRDHOUSE REPEAT PATTERN

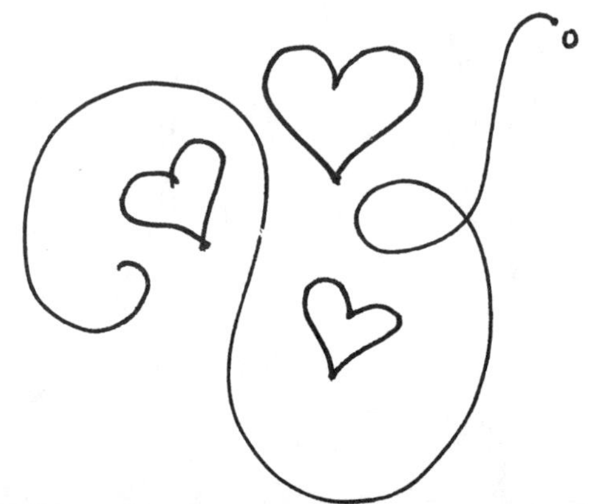

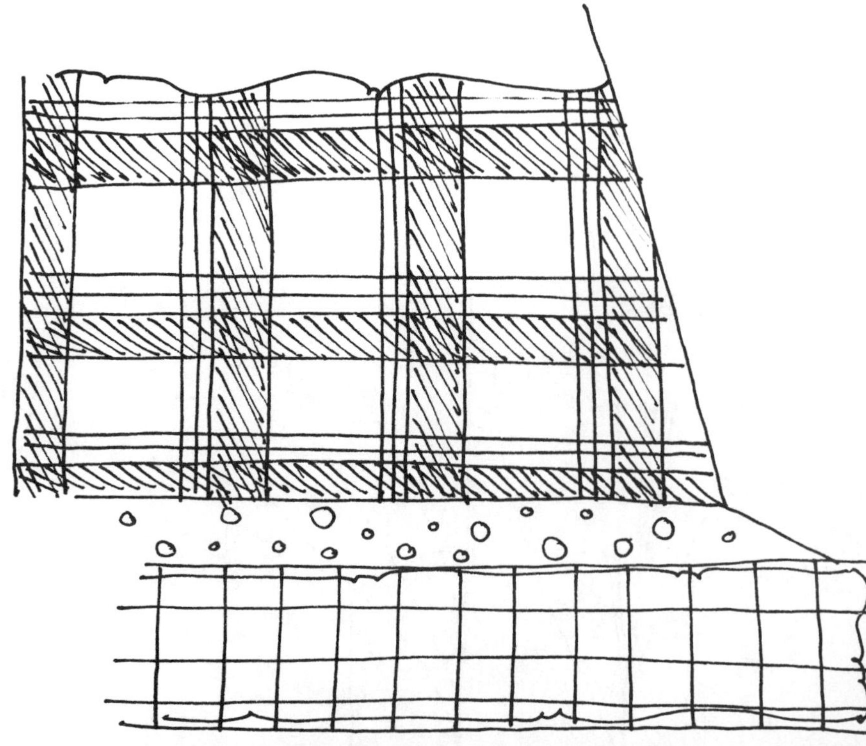

MAIL BOX BIRDHOUSE

DecoArt Americana Colors:

DA164 Lt. Buttermilk
DA7 Moon Yellow
DA41 Country Blue
DA27 Gooseberry Pink
DA52 Avocado

DecoArt Patio Paint:

DCP18 Woodland Brown

DecoArt Specialty Products:

DS18 Multi Purpose
DAS13 Matte Spray

Surfaces by DC&C

Mailbox Birdhouse #28-0183
Tin-tiques:
Bird #24-7127
Watering Can #24-7129

Miscellaneous Supplies:

Yellow Checked Wired Ribbon
Hot Glue Gun
Spanish Moss

Painting Instructions:

1. Apply one even coat of **Multi Purpose Sealer** to all tin pieces.
2. Basecoat in **Moon Yellow.**
3. Stripe top and do checks on bottom in **Lt. Buttermilk**.
4. Blue flowers and thin lines, mix of 1 part **Lt. Buttermilk** to 1 part **Country Blue**.
5. Pink flowers and thin lines, and dots mix of 1 part **Gooseberry Pink** to 1 part **Lt. Buttermilk**. Do accent dots by flowers in **Lt. Buttermilk**.
6. Leaves and stems **Avocado**.
7. Liner-work **Black**.
8. Apply an even coat of Matte Spray and antique with **Woodland Brown**.

To Finish:

Glue bow and tin pieces in place. Spatter piece with **Black** and re-spray.

MAIL BOX BIRDHOUSE REPEAT PATTERN

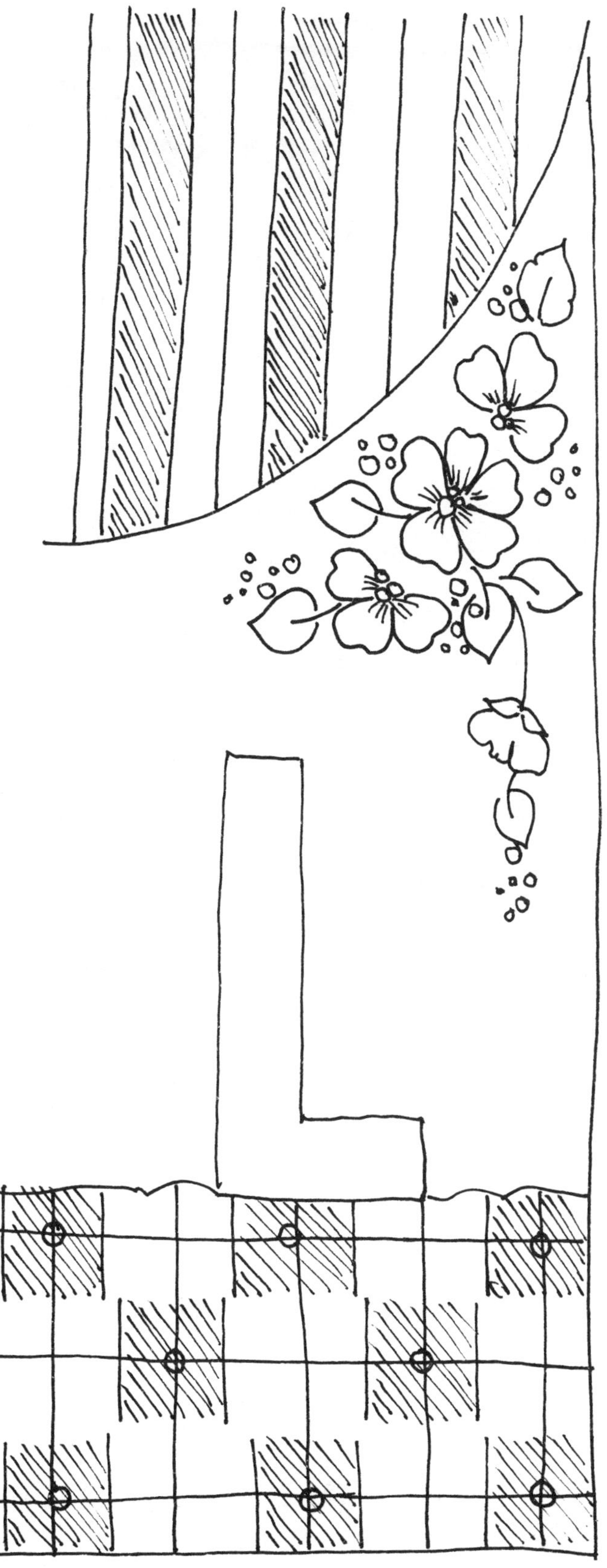

APPLES & STARS
TALL BOX
REPEAT PATTERN

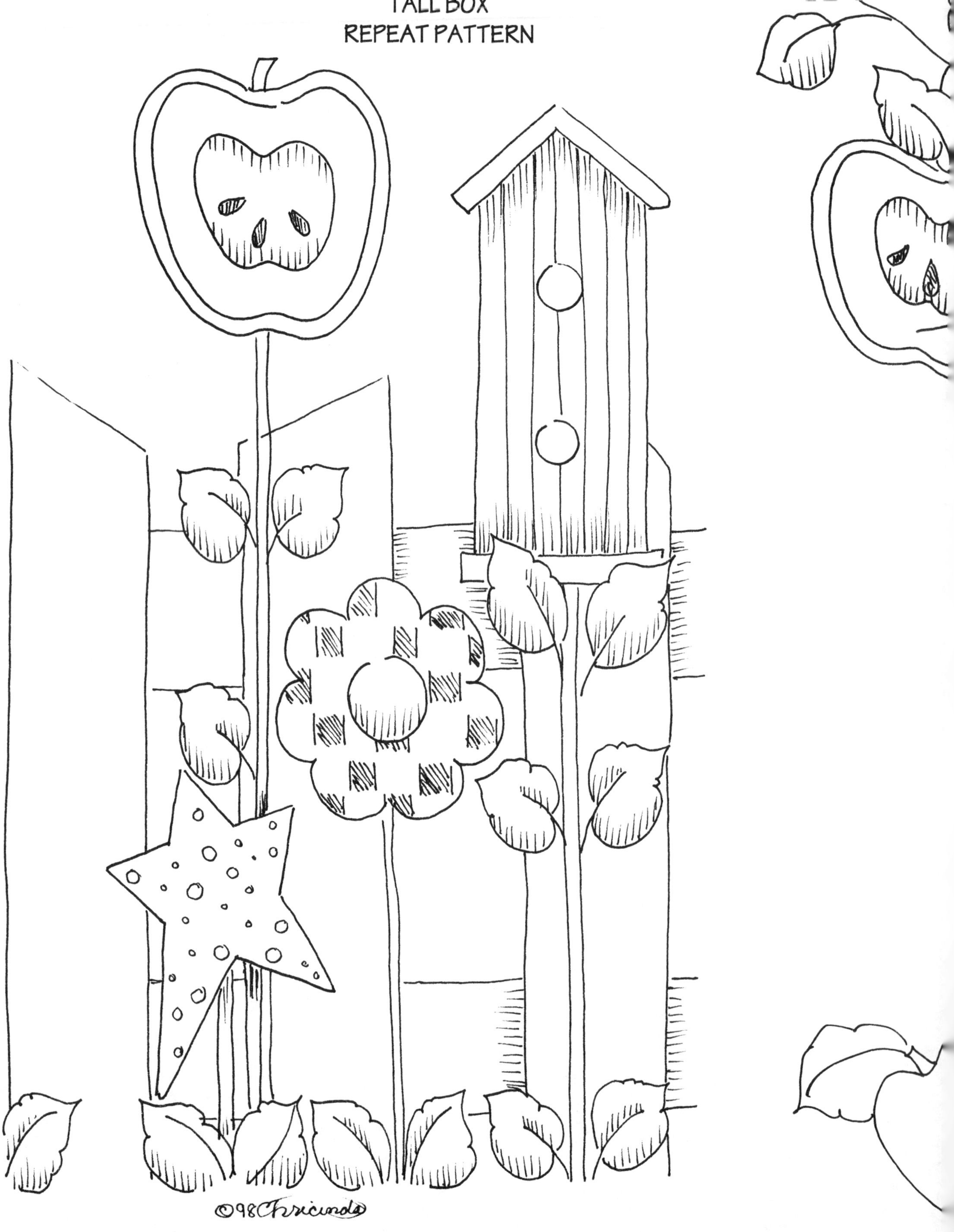

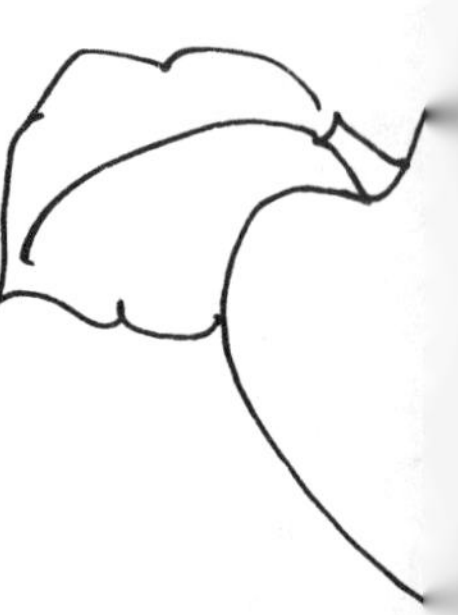

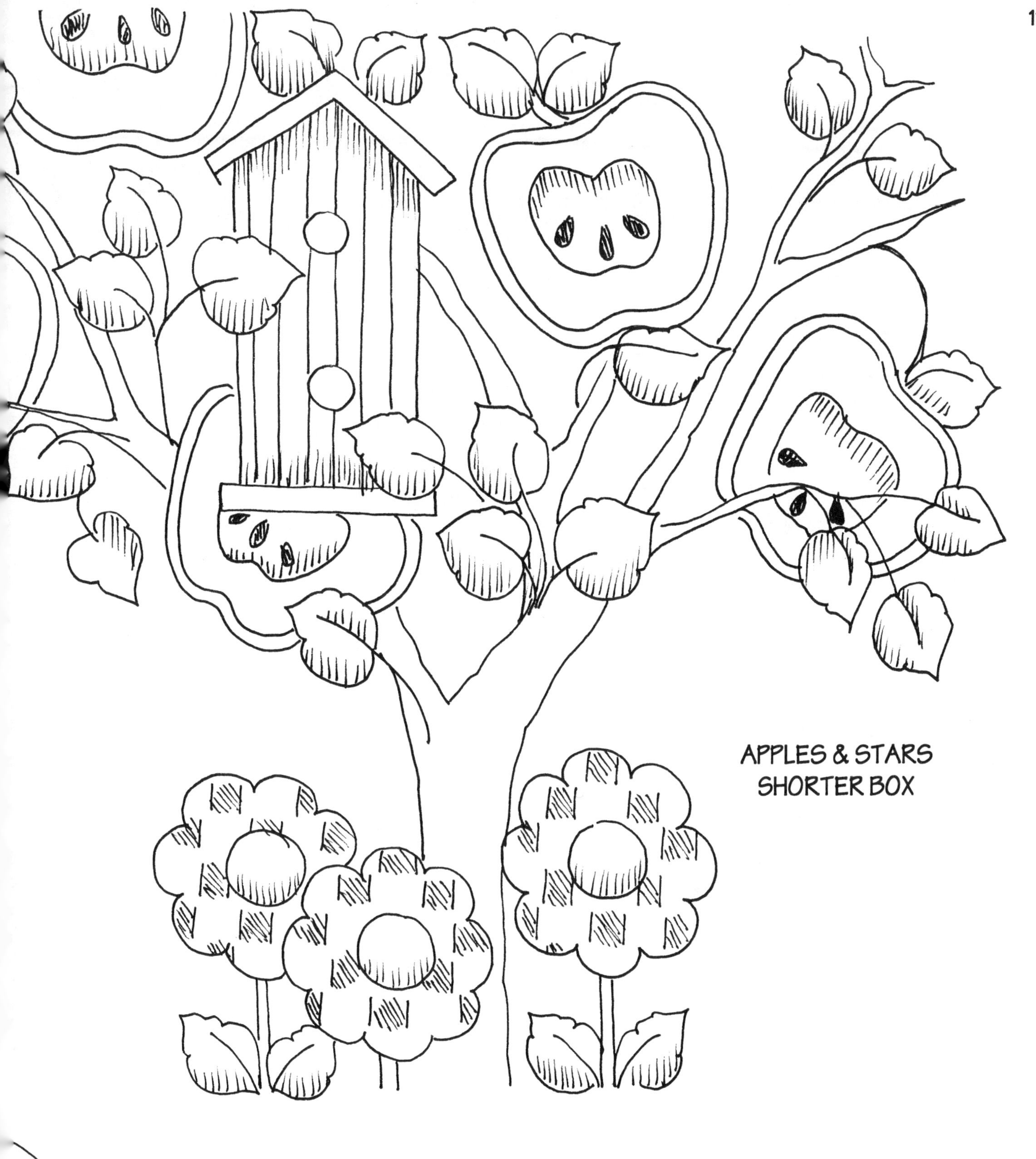

APPLES & STARS
SHORTER BOX

WHAT ARE THE THREE BEST THINGS ABOUT BEING A TEACHER? JUNE, JULY & AUGUST!

APPLES AND STARS
Antiqued Watering Can, Plant Tray, and Two Tall Boxes

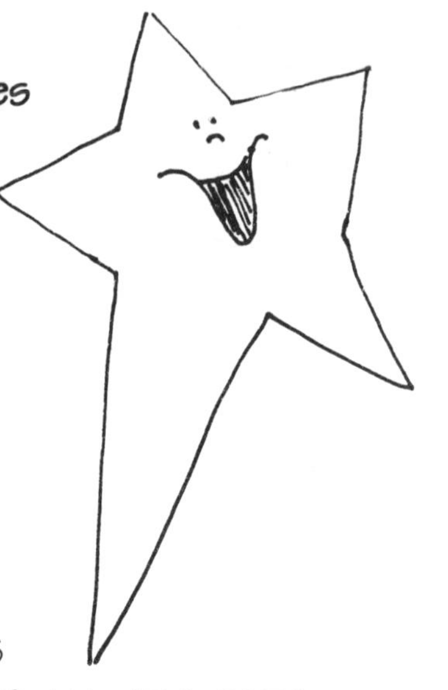

DecoArt Americana Colors:

DA67 Black
DA166 Deep Midnight Blue
DA7 Moon Yellow
DA160 Antique Maroon
DA51 Leaf Green
DA86 Uniform Blue
DA3 Buttermilk
DA18 Country Red
DA62 Terra-cotta
DA173 Khaki Tan
DA133 Hauser Dark Green
DA194 Marigold

DecoArt Patio Paints

DCP04 Pine Green
DCP18 Woodland Brown

DecoArt Specialty Product:

DS4 Decorating Paste
DAS13 Matte Spray
DS17 Multi Purpose Sealer

Surfaces by DC&C

Watering Can #28-4101
Large Oval Tray #28-3956
Tall Square Boxes w/ Rusty Tin Lids #28-9239

Miscellaneous Supplies:

Compressed Sponge
Seawool Sponge
Paper Ribbon
Raffia
Glue Gun

Painting Instructions all four Pieces:

1. Tape off below or above the green areas on all pieces. With a palette knife apply Decorating Paste. When dry remove tape. With a seawool sponge apply **Decorating Paste** to the light areas.
2. Basecoat the green areas in **Leaf Green**, dry-brush with **Buttermilk** plus a touch of **Leaf Green.** Antique with **Pine Green.**
3. Basecoat the light areas in a mix of 2 parts **Khaki Tan** to 1 part **Buttermilk.**

Two Tall Boxes:

1. On the large box basecoat the picket fence in Buttermilk. Float the shadows with **Terra-cotta.**
2. On the small box basecoat the tree trunk in **Terra-cotta.** Float the shadows with **Antique Maroon.**

On Watering Can and 2 Tall Boxes:

3. Basecoat the apples in **Buttermilk.** Float the shadows with **Terra-cotta.** Do the skin in **Country Red.** Do the seeds and the stems in **Antique Maroon.**
4. Basecoat the birdhouse in **Uniform Blue.** Stripe with **Buttermilk** plus a touch of **Leaf Green.** Do the porch and roof in **Antique Maroon.**
5. Basecoat the flower in **Moon Yellow.** Do the checks with **Marigold** plus a touch of **Terra-cotta.** Float the shadows with **Marigold.** Do centers with **Antique Maroon.**

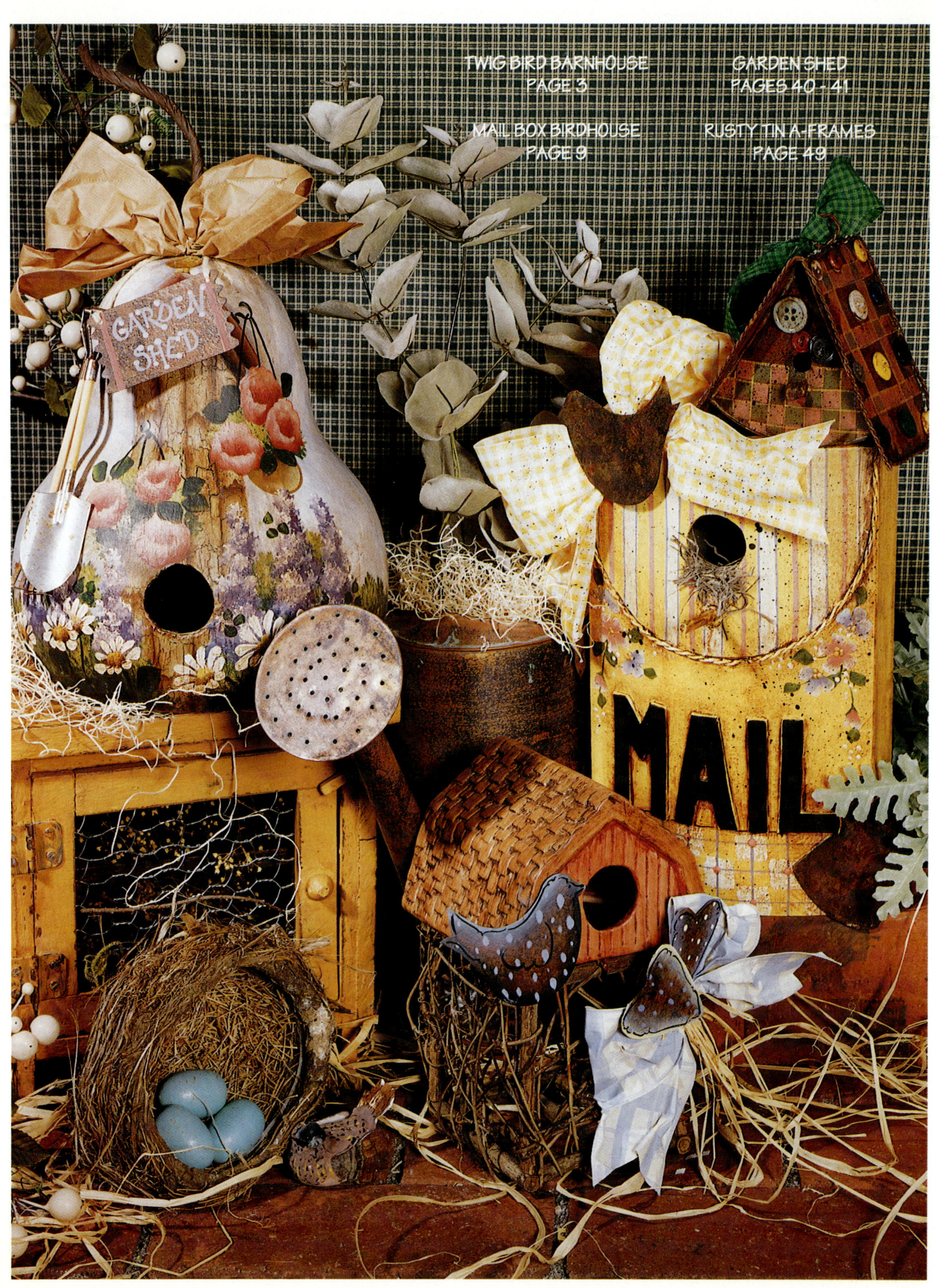

TWIG BIRD BARNHOUSE
PAGE 3

GARDEN SHED
PAGES 40 - 41

MAIL BOX BIRDHOUSE
PAGE 9

RUSTY TIN A-FRAMES
PAGE 49

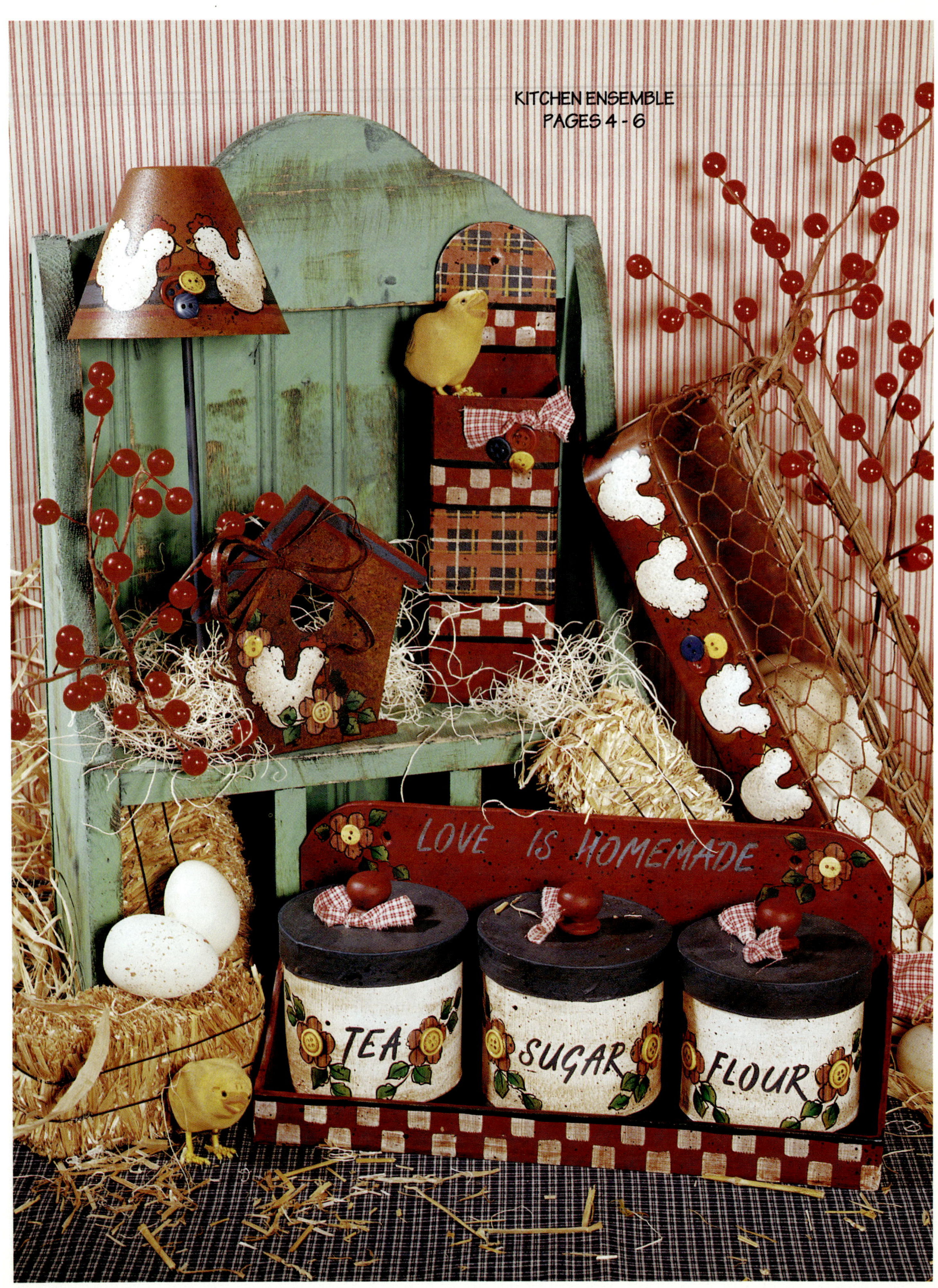

KITCHEN ENSEMBLE
PAGES 4 - 6

6. Do all leaves in **Leaf Green** plus a touch of **Hauser Dark Green**.
7. Basecoat the stars in **Terra-cotta.** Dot with **Marigold.** Float the shadows with **Country Red.**
8. Band in **Terra-cotta.**
9. Apply one even coat of **Multi Purpose Sealer** to the lids of the boxes and check with **Moon Yellow** tipped in **Buttermilk.**

Plant Tray:

1. Cut 3/4 " check from compressed sponge. Check the entire light area **Terra-cotta** tipped in **Antique Maroon.**
2. Basecoat the flowers in **Moon Yellow**. Stripe with **Uniform Blue.** Float the shadows with **Marigold.** Do centers with **Antique Maroon.**
3. Stroke the leaves with a mix of **Leaf Green** plus a touch of **Hauser Dark Green.**

To Finish all Pieces:

1. Do all liner-work and spatter with **Black.**
2. Spray with **Matte Spray** and antique with **Woodland Brown.**
3. Glue raffia and bow in place according to color picture.

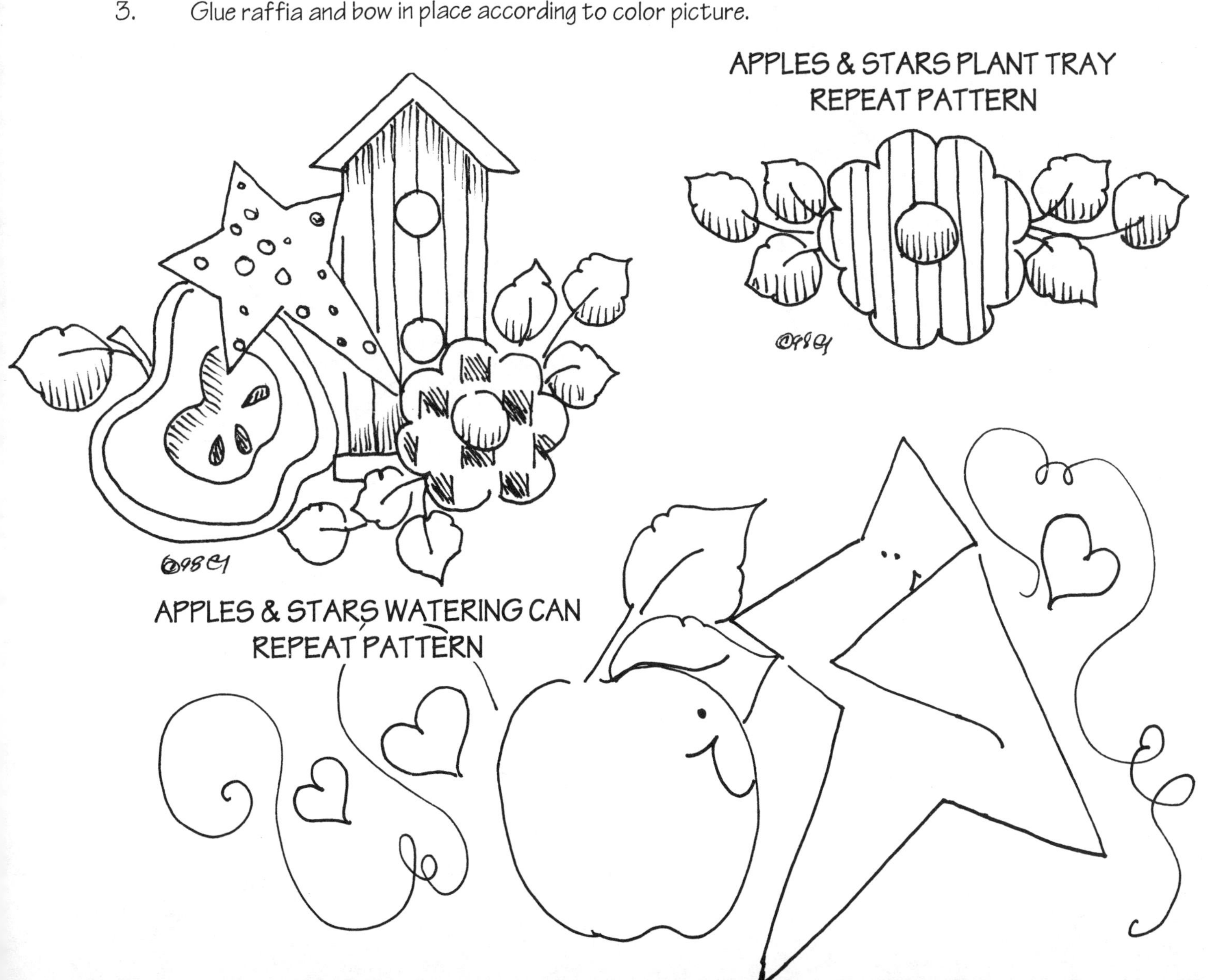

WEATHERED WOOD FOR DAD

Duck Basket &Tin Rimmed Boxes, Wire Pitcher, and Gourd

DecoArt Americana Colors:

- DA67 Black
- DA153 Egg Shell
- DA100 Ultra Deep Blue
- DA1 White
- DA112 Cranberry Wine
- DA158 Antique Teal
- DA194 Marigold
- DA107 Teal Green
- DA65 Dk. Chocolate

DecoArt Patio Paint:

- DCP18 Woodland Brown

DecoArt Specialty Product:

- DAS8 Weathered Wood
- DS17 Multi Purpose Sealer

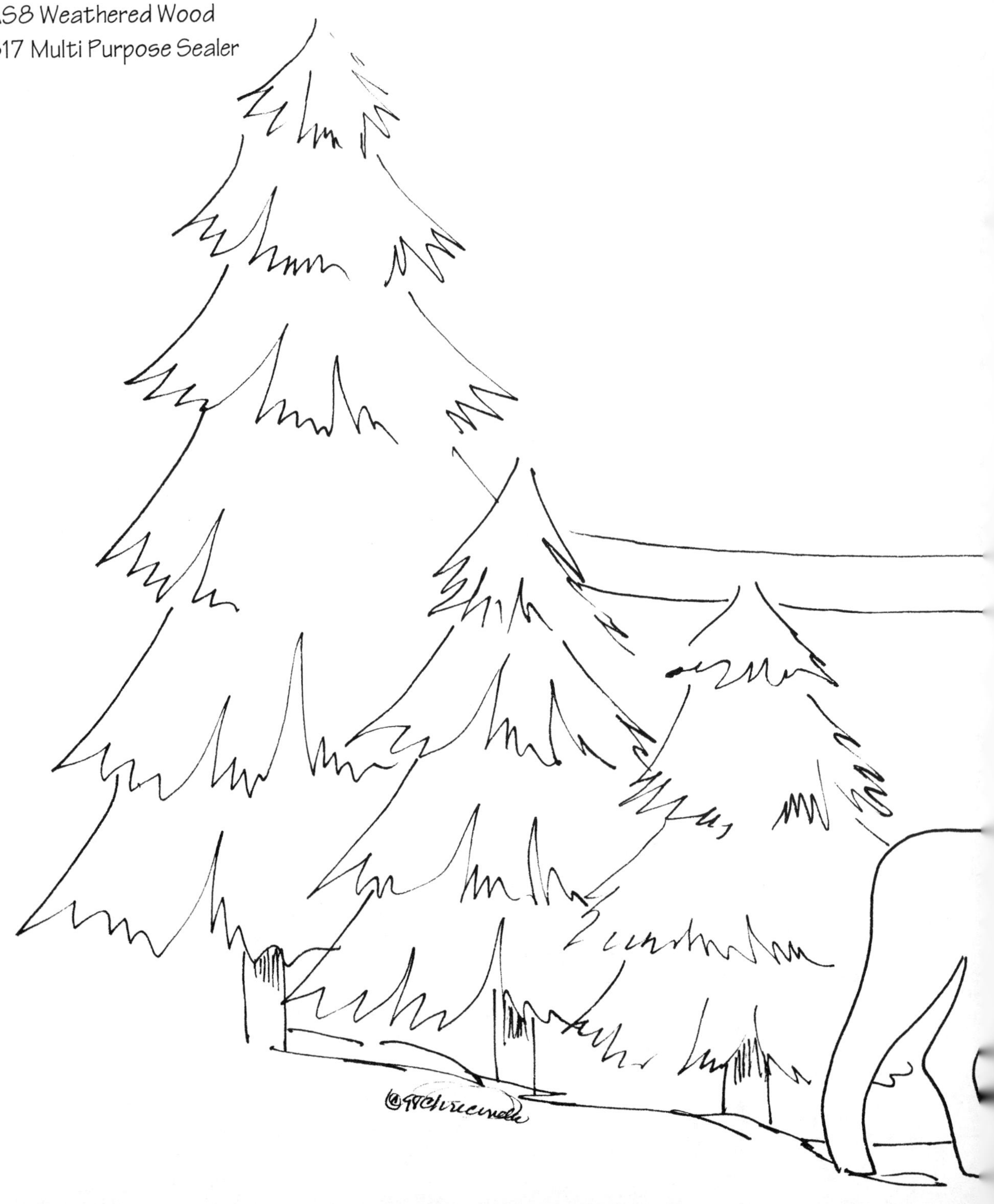

Surfaces by DC&C

Lg. Round Boxes With Rusty Tin Band #28-9183
Duck Basket #28-3893
Pot Bellies Gourd #28-0205
Two Bears #24-7132
Three Trees #24-7145
Rusty Tin Pitcher #24-7401
Tin-tiques
Four Moose #24-7131
Two Fish #24-7130

Miscellaneous Supplies:

Raffia
Tacky Glue
Glue Gun
Ribbon
Wire

Painting Instructions for all pieces:

1. Basecoat all pieces except tin in **Black**. Apply one coat of **Weathered Wood.** Allow to dry and apply one heavy coat of **Eggshell.**
2. Apply one even coat of **Multi Purpose Sealer** to all tin.

For Boxes:

1. Do large bands in **Cranberry Wine.** On small box stripe the large band first with **Ultra Deep Blue,** float the shadows on this with **Ultra Deep Blue** plus a touch of **Black,** float the highlights with **White** plus a touch of **Ultra Deep Blue.** Do narrow stripes in **Teal Green** and **Marigold.**
2. On the middle box do the small horizontal stripes in **Teal Green.** Band edge of large band with **Ultra Deep Blue,** float the shadows on this with **Ultra Deep Blue** plus a touch of **Black,** float the highlights with **White** plus a touch of **Ultra Deep Blue.** Do the rick-rack with **Marigold.**
3. On large box do diagonal stripes in **Ultra Deep Blue,** float the shadows on this with **Ultra Deep Blue** plus a touch of **Black,** float the highlights with **White** plus a touch of **Ultra Deep Blue,** medium stripe Teal Green, narrow Marigold.

WEATHERED WOOD FOR DAD
DUCK BASKET

WEATHERED WOOD FOR DAD Continued

Duck Basket:

1. Dry-brush the breast area in **Cranberry Wine**, head in **Antique Teal**, beak **Marigold**, ring around neck **White**. Eye **Black**, highlights **Marigold**. Do band around basket in **Cranberry Wine** and on each side of this with **Ultra Deep Blue** plus a touch of **Black**.

Spruce:

1. Basecoat the blue spruce in **Antique Teal**. Float the shadows with **Black** and the highlights with **White** plus a touch of **Teal Green**. Do the trunks in **Dk. Chocolate** side loaded with **Marigold**.
2. Float the ground at the bottom of the trees with **Dk. Chocolate.**
3. Float the water with **Ultra Deep Blue, White** and **Black** working wet in wet.

Wire Pitcher:

To do plaid do all horizontal and then vertical in **Russet**, **Teal Green** and **Marigold**. Then do vertical and horizontal **Ultra Deep Blue** plus a touch of **Black**.

Gourd:

1. Basecoat the flowers in **Cranberry Wine** plus a touch of **Eggshell**. Float the shadows with **Cranberry Wine** plus a touch of **Black**, and the highlights with **Eggshell** plus a touch of **Cranberry Wine**. Stipple the centers with **Marigold** tipped in **Dk. Chocolate**. Basecoat the stem in **Dk. Chocolate.**
2. Stroke the leaves in **Antique Teal**. Do all tole strokes in **Ultra Deep Blue**.

To Finish all Pieces:

1. Antique with **Woodland Brown**.
2. Glue on tin pieces, then bows.

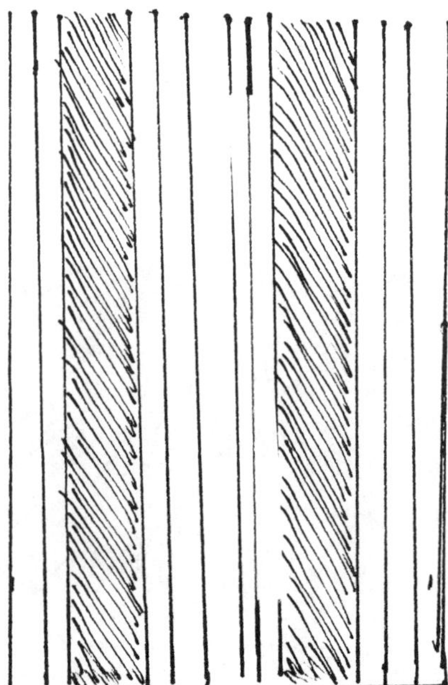

WEATHERED WOOD FOR DAD
BOXES REPEAT PATTERN

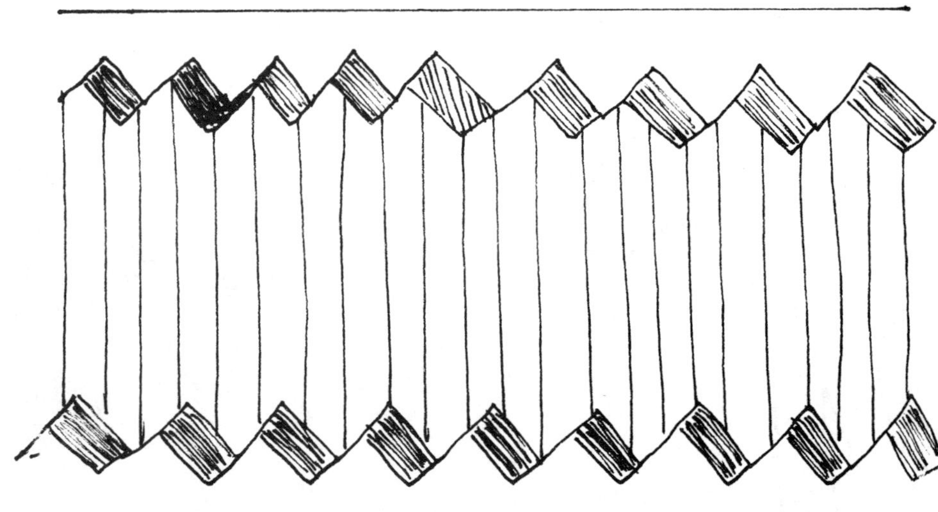

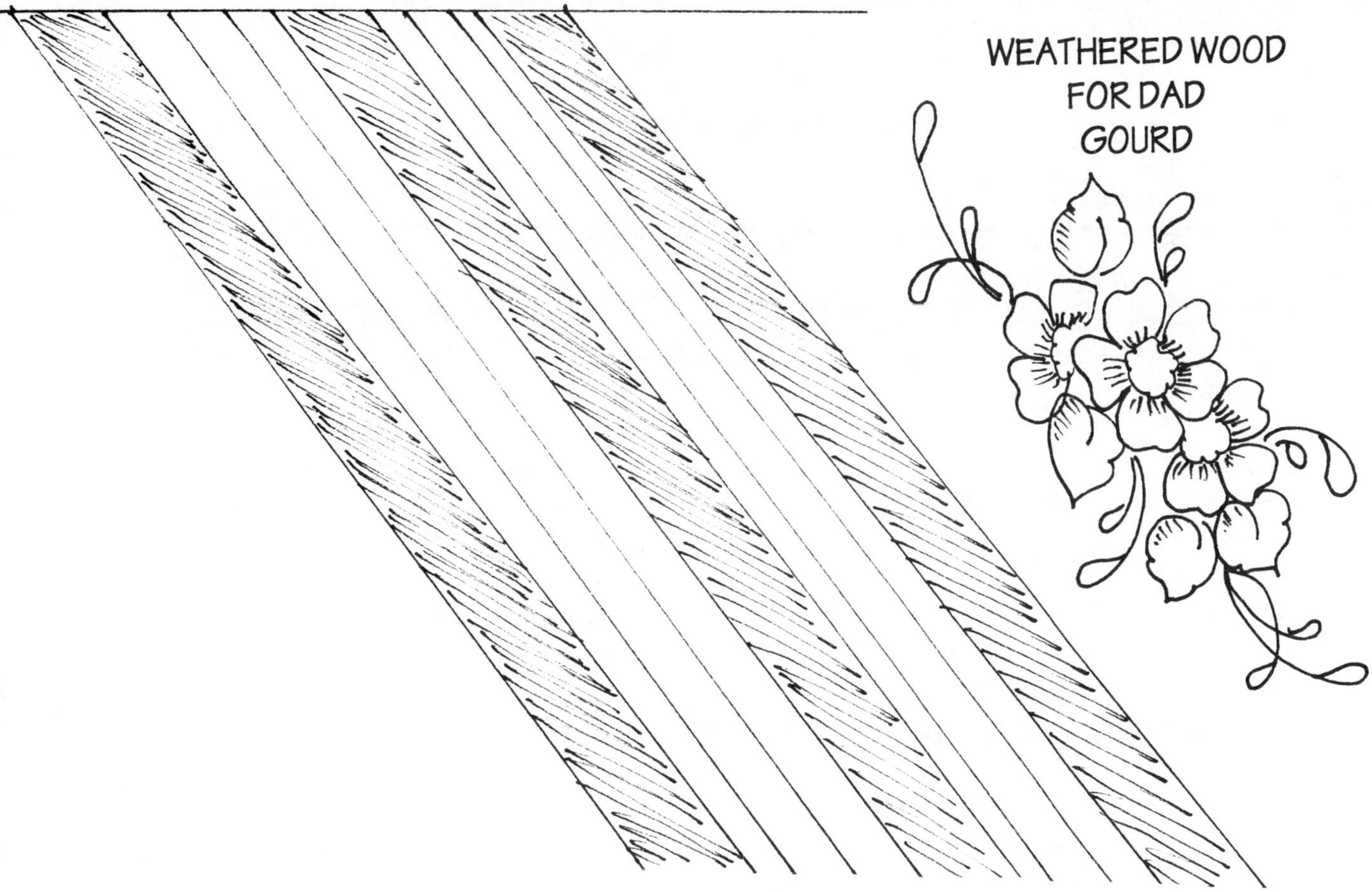

WEATHERED WOOD
FOR DAD
GOURD

WEATHERED WOOD FOR DAD
BOXES REPEAT PATTERN

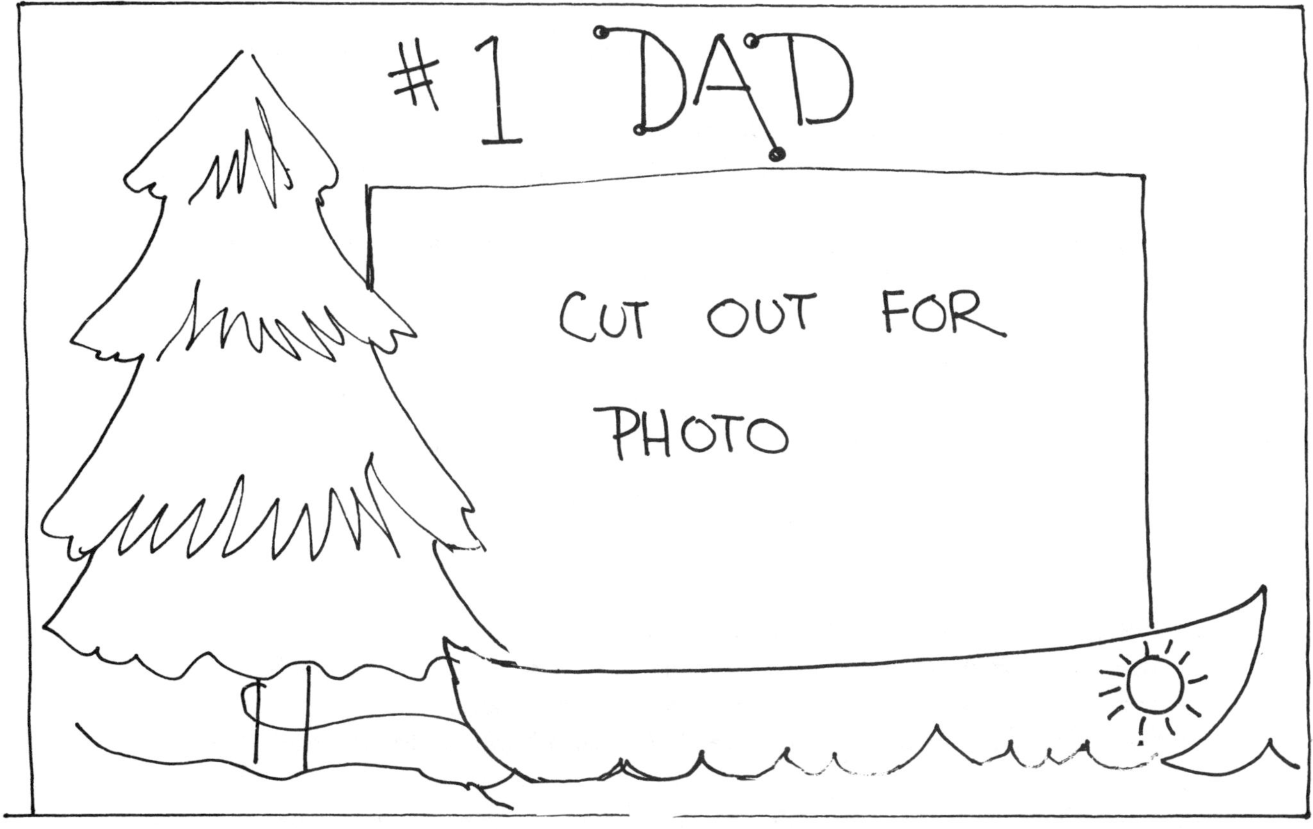

SPRING ANGEL
Tintique Pocket, Watering Can

DecoArt Americana Colors

DA184 French Vanilla
DA57 Jade Green
DA168 Golden Straw
DA154 Pansy Lavender
DS18 Multi Purpose Sealer
DA189 Summer Lilac
DA60 Mocha
DA67 Black
DA52 Avocado
DA1 White
DA156 Antique Rose
DA65 Dk. Chocolate
DA71 Glorious Gold

Surface by DC&C

Large Oval Boxes #28-0015
Rusty Tin Diamond Pocket #24-7380
Watering Can #28-4212
Tin-tique:
2 Folk Art Birds#24-7127
Two Watering Cans #24-7129
One Primitive Heart #24-7213

Miscellaneous Supplies:

Lavender Checked Wired Paper Ribbon
Compressed Sponge
Raffia
Glue Gun
Yellow Daisies
Buttons
Tacky Glue

Cut all pieces of compressed sponge.

Painting Instructions for Angel:

1. Apply one even coat of Multi Purpose Sealer to all tin pieces.
2. Basecoat the 2 bottom boxes in **French Vanilla.**
3. Sponge flowers **Antique Rose** tipped in **White, Golden Straw** tipped in **White, Pansy Lavender** tipped in **White.** Stipple the centers in **French Vanilla.**
4. Do the stems in **Avocado.** Sponge leaves in **Avocado** tipped in **Jade Green.**
5. On the middle box to do the plaid thin to the consistency of heavy cream **Summer Lilac** plus a touch of **Pansy Lavender, White,** and **Avocado.** Do the horizontal and then the vertical. Basecoat the lid in the **Summer Lilac** and **Pansy Lavender** mix. Check with **White.**
6. Basecoat her face in **Mocha.** Basecoat her hair in **Dk. Chocolate.** Float her cheeks with **Antique Rose** plus a touch of **Mocha.** Streak her hair with **Golden Straw** plus a touch of **White.**
7. Accent tin pieces with the lavender mix and **Golden Straw** plus a touch of **French Vanilla.**
8. Basecoat her halo in **Glorious Gold.** Do all liner work **Black.**

To Finish:

With tacky glue apply tin pieces. Make wings and bow from lavender checked ribbon, glue in place. Make raffia bows and glue in place.

Painting Instructions For Spring Pocket and Spring Watering Can:

1. On watering can basecoat the **Jade Green** and dot with **Buttermilk.** Basecoat the **Buttermilk** areas.
2. Sponge checks with **Pansy Lavender** tipped in **White.**
3. Sponge flowers in **Antique Rose** tipped in **White, Golden Straw** tipped in **White,** or **Pansy Lavender** tipped in **White.** Stipple the centers in **French Vanilla.**
4. Do the stems in **Avocado.** Sponge leaves in **Avocado** tipped in **Jade Green.**

To Finish:

Make bow from lavender checked ribbon, glue in place. Make raffia bows and glue in place. Apply buttons.

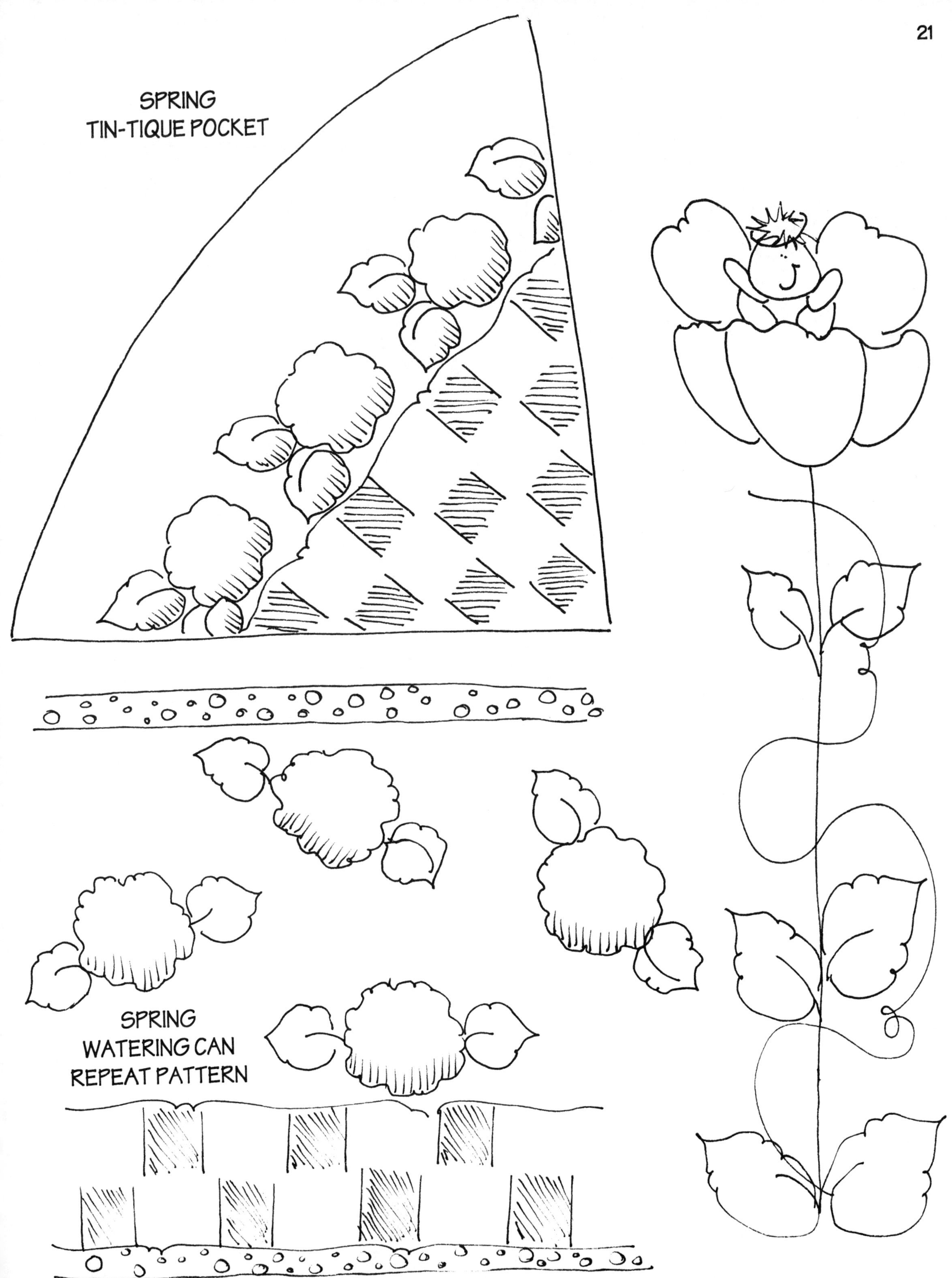
SPRING
TIN-TIQUE POCKET
SPRING
WATERING CAN
REPEAT PATTERN

SPRING SPONGE PATTERNS

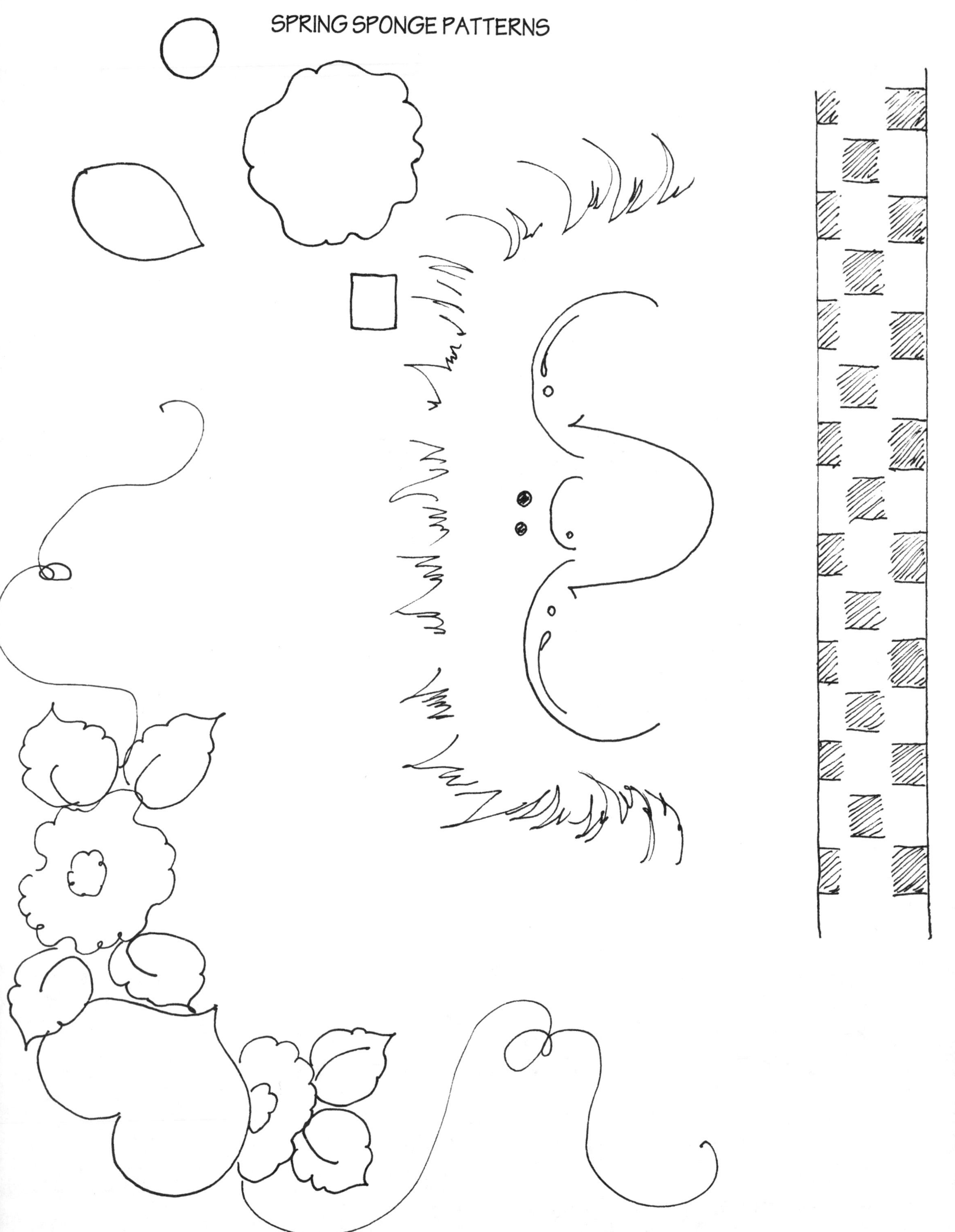

SPRING ANGEL
REPEAT PATTERN

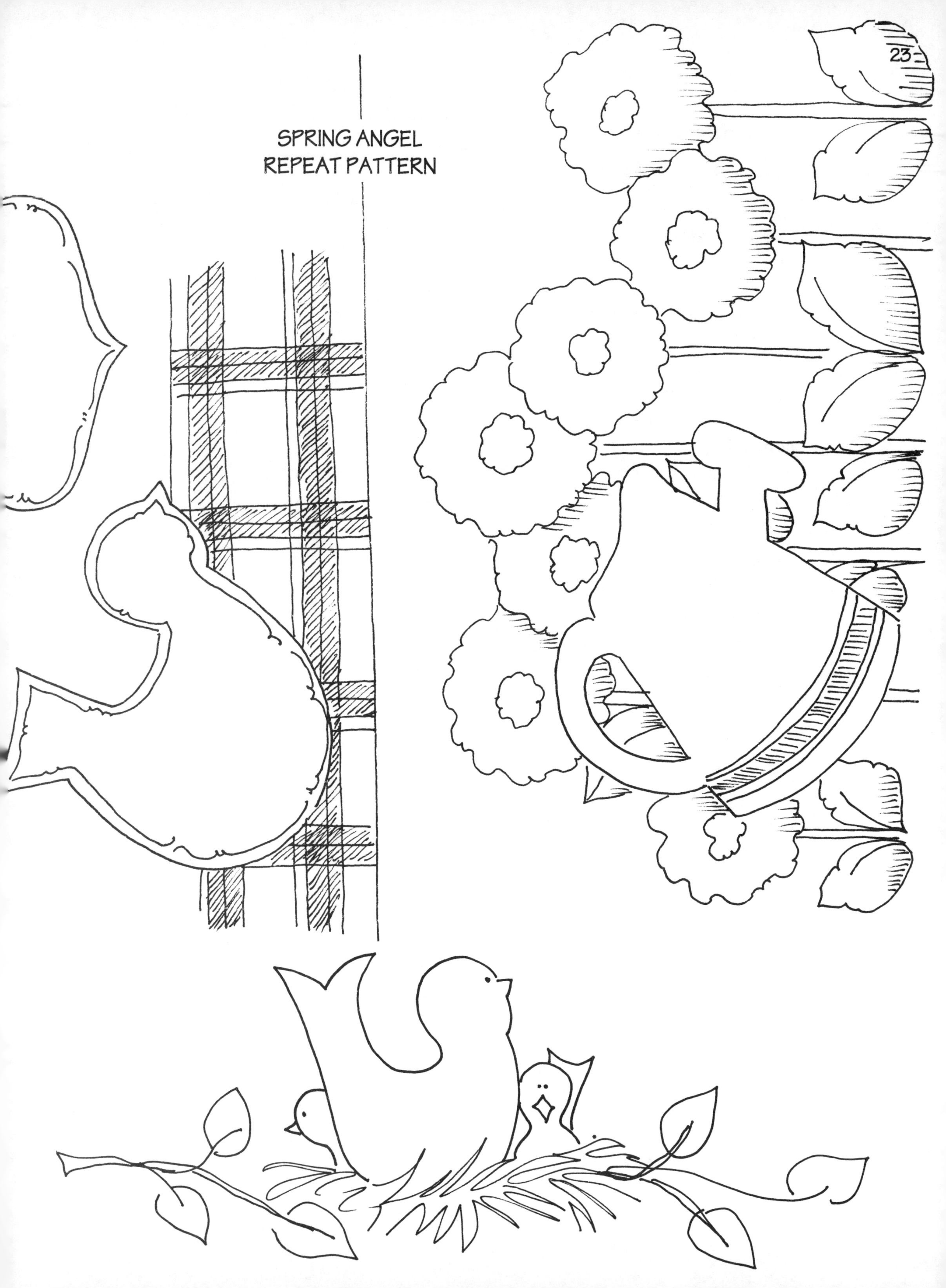

RUSTY TIN BUNNY SILHOUETTE

DecoArt Americana Colors

DA184 French Vanilla
DA189 Summer Lilac
DA1 White
DA57 Jade Green
DA186 French Mauve
DA150 Royal Purple
DA168 Golden Straw
DA67 Black
DA162 Antique Mauve
DA52 Avocado
DS18 Multi-Purpose sealer

Surface by DC&C

Rusty Tin Bunny Silhouette #24-7354

Miscellaneous Supplies:

Compressed Sponge

Painting Instructions:

1. Cut all pieces of compressed sponge.
2. Apply one even coat of **Multi Purpose Sealer** to the entire piece.
3. Apply tulips in **Antique Mauve** tipped in **French Mauve, Golden Straw** tipped in **French Vanilla** or **Royal Purple** tipped in **Summer Lilac** and a touch of **White.**
4. Apply stems in **Avocado.** Apply leaves in **Avocado** tipped in **Jade Green.**
5. Do all linerwork in **Black.**

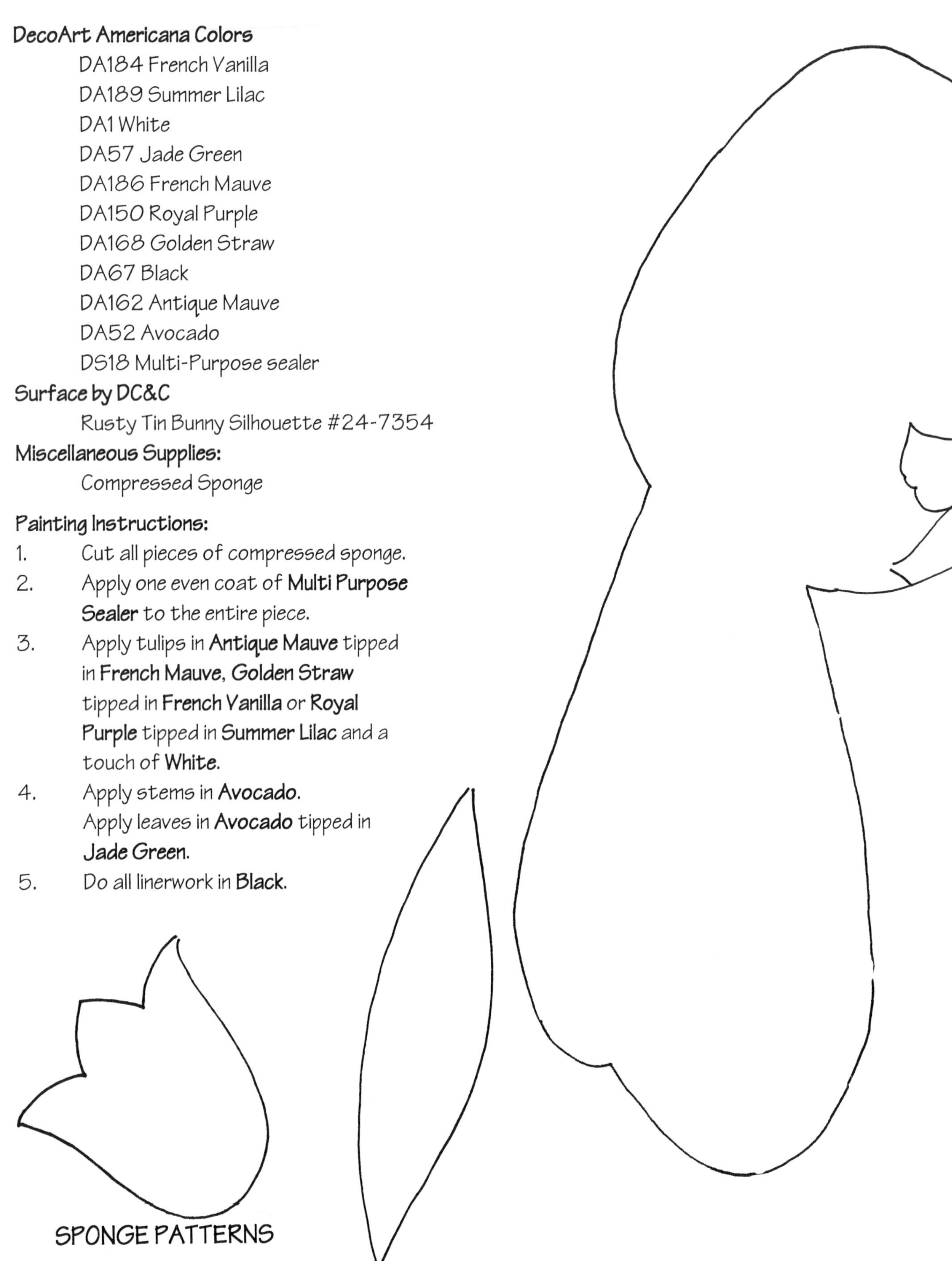

SPONGE PATTERNS

RUSTY TIN BUNNY SILHOUETTE

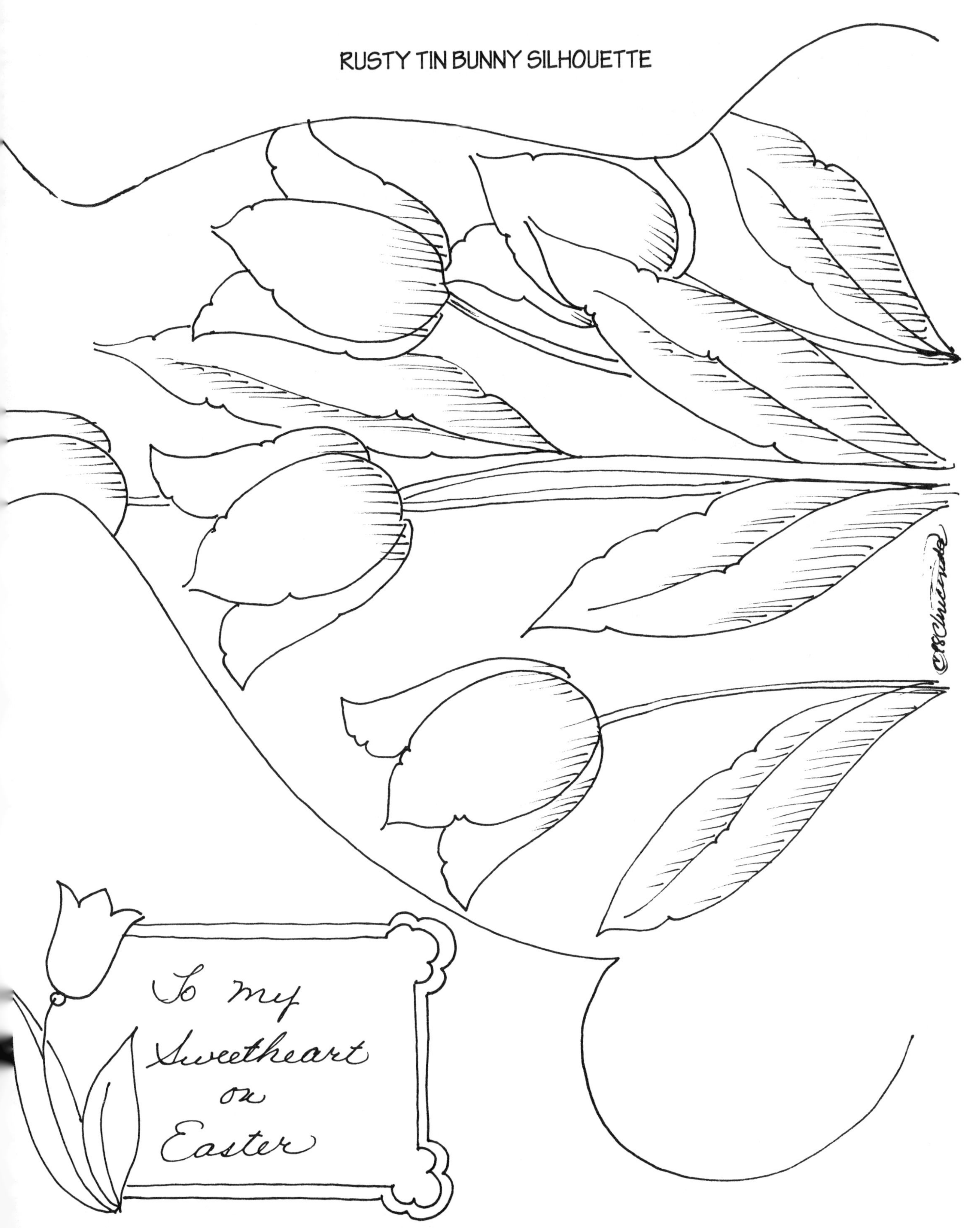

BEDROOM ENSEMBLE

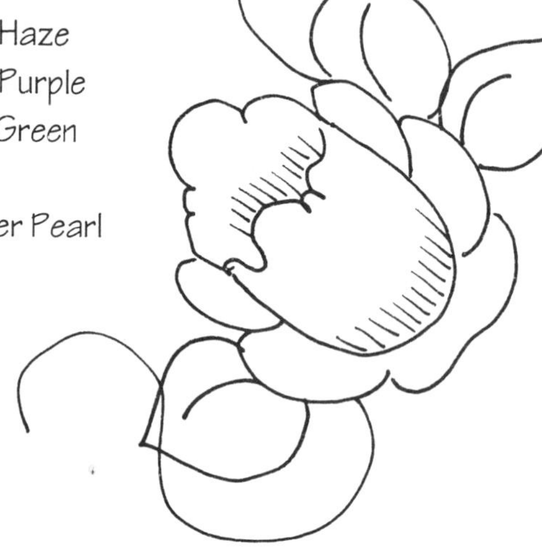

DecoArt Americana Acrylics:

DA111 Grey Sky
DA195 Bittersweet Chocolate
DA67 Black
DA52 Avocado
DA28 Raspberry
DA141 Blue Violet
DA163 Honey Brown
DA112 Cranberry Wine
DA1 White
DA168 Golden Straw
DA57 Jade Green
DA197 Violet Haze
DA150 Royal Purple
DA157 Black Green

DecoArt Dazzling Metallics:

DA204 Pewter
DA73 Bronze
DA203 Oyster Pearl

DecoArt Specialty Products:

DS18 Multi Purpose Sealer
DAS13 Matte Spray
DS18 Faux Glaze Medium

Surfaces by DC&C

Tapered Container #28-4005
Oval Box Rusty Tin Lid #28-9223
Two Candle Lamp Shade Holders #29-5152
Two Metal w/Brown Paper Lamp Shades #29-5161
Rusty Tin Cat Silhouette #24-7355
9" Embossed Square Box #28-4274
Candle Holders #29-5178 and #29-5177

Miscellaneous Supplies:

Plastic Wrap

Base Painting Instructions For all Pieces:

1. Basecoat all of the blue areas on all pieces in **Grey Sky** plus a touch of **Pewter**. The mottled areas on the blue are done with a mix of equal parts **Faux Glaze Medium** and **Pewter**, working one area at a time, apply an even coat, while still wet lay on plastic wrap and lift.
2. Basecoat the brown areas in a mix of 3 parts **Bronze** to 1 part **Bittersweet Chocolate**. On the bottom of the waste basket apply a mix of equal parts **Faux Glaze Medium** to **Bittersweet Chocolate**, while still wet lay on plastic wrap and lift. On the embossed areas of the square box antique with this mix.

Wastebasket:

1. Double load the round brush and stroke pink flowers in **Raspberry** tipped in **White.** Float the shadows with **Cranberry Wine**. Blue flowers are **Violet Haze** tipped in **White**. Float the shadows with **Blue Violet** plus a touch of **Royal Purple**. Yellow flowers are **Golden Straw** tipped in **White**, float shadows with **Honey Brown**.

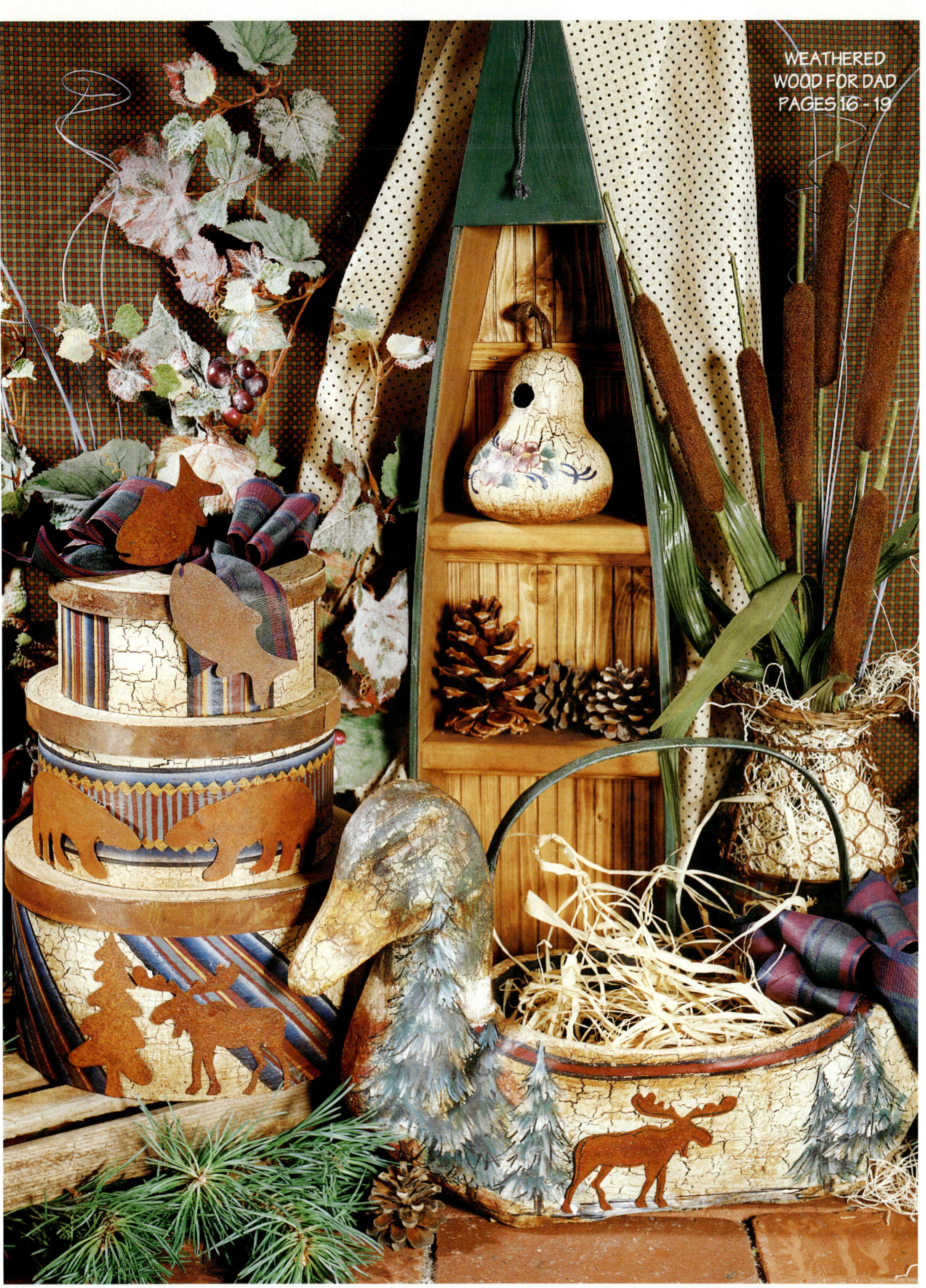
WEATHERED
WOOD FOR DAD
PAGES 16 - 19

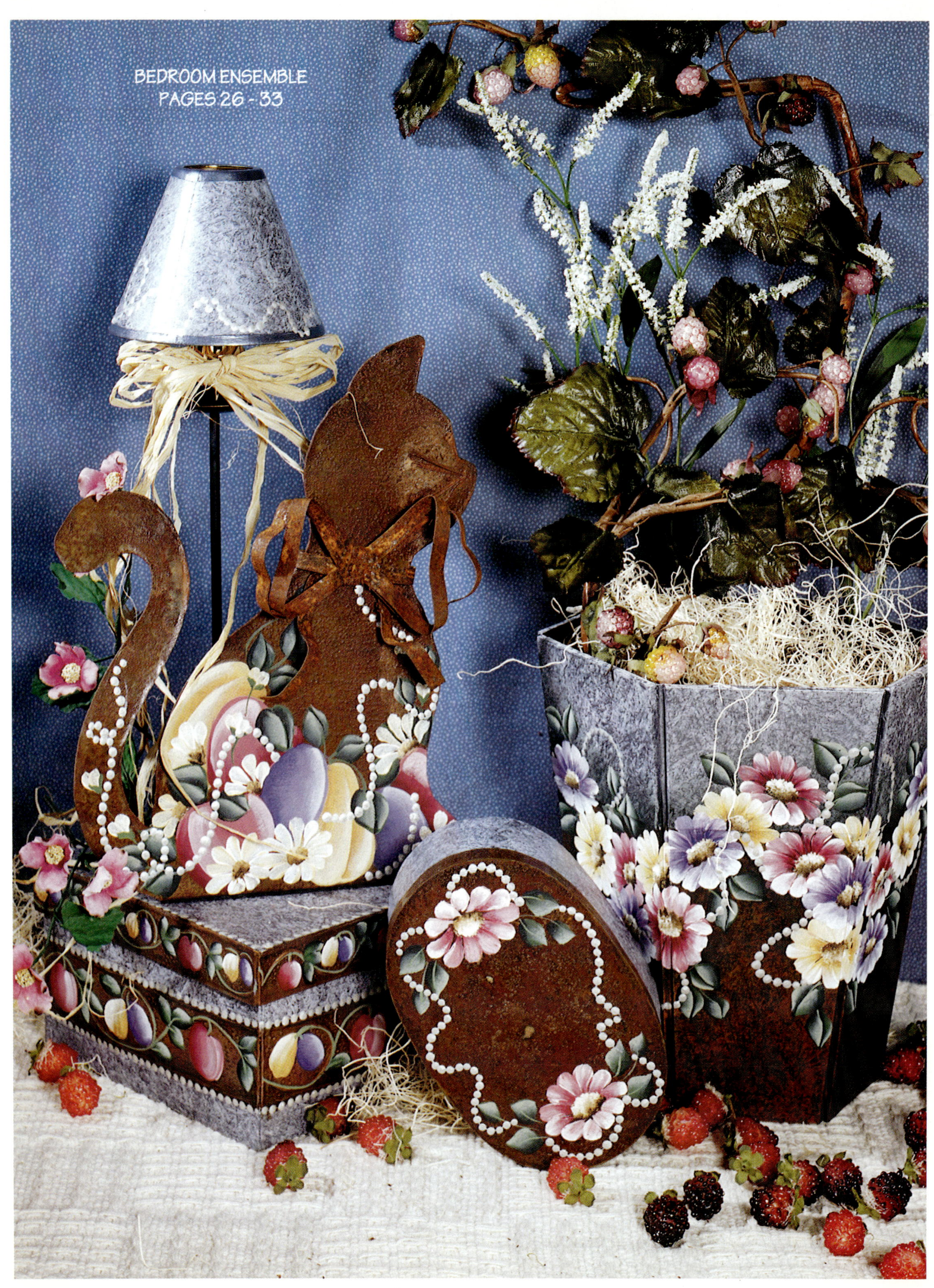
BEDROOM ENSEMBLE
PAGES 26 - 33

2. Stipple the centers with **Honey Brown** tipped in **White**. Float shadows with **Bittersweet Chocolate**.
3. Stroke the leaves in **Avocado**, float the shadows with **Black Green** and the highlights with **Jade Green**.
4. Dot string of pearls with **Oyster Pearl**.

Embossed Box: Because of the embossing there is no pattern for this box.

1. Basecoat all leaves in **Avocado**, float shadows **Black Green** and highlights with **Jade Green**.
2. Basecoat plums in **Violet Haze**. Float shadows with **Blue Violet** plus a touch of **Royal Purple**, and highlights with **White** plus a touch of **Violet Haze**.
3. Basecoat apples in **Raspberry**. Float shadows with **Cranberry Wine** and highlights with **White** plus a touch of **Raspberry**.
4. Basecoat yellow fruit in **Golden Straw**. Float the shadows with **Honey Brown** and the highlights with **White** plus a touch of **Golden Straw**.

Tin Lid Oval Box:

Apply one even coat of **Multi Purpose Sealer** to tin lid. Follow steps Nos. 1-4 of wastebasket using only pink flower.

Lamp Shades:

Band with **Pewter**. Dot with **Oyster Pearl**.

Tin Cat Silhouette:

Follow instructions for embossed box fruit #1-4. Do the daisies in strokes of **Golden Straw** tipped in **White**. Stipple the centers in **Honey Brown** and float shadows with **Bittersweet**.

Paint pearls with **Oyster Pearl**.

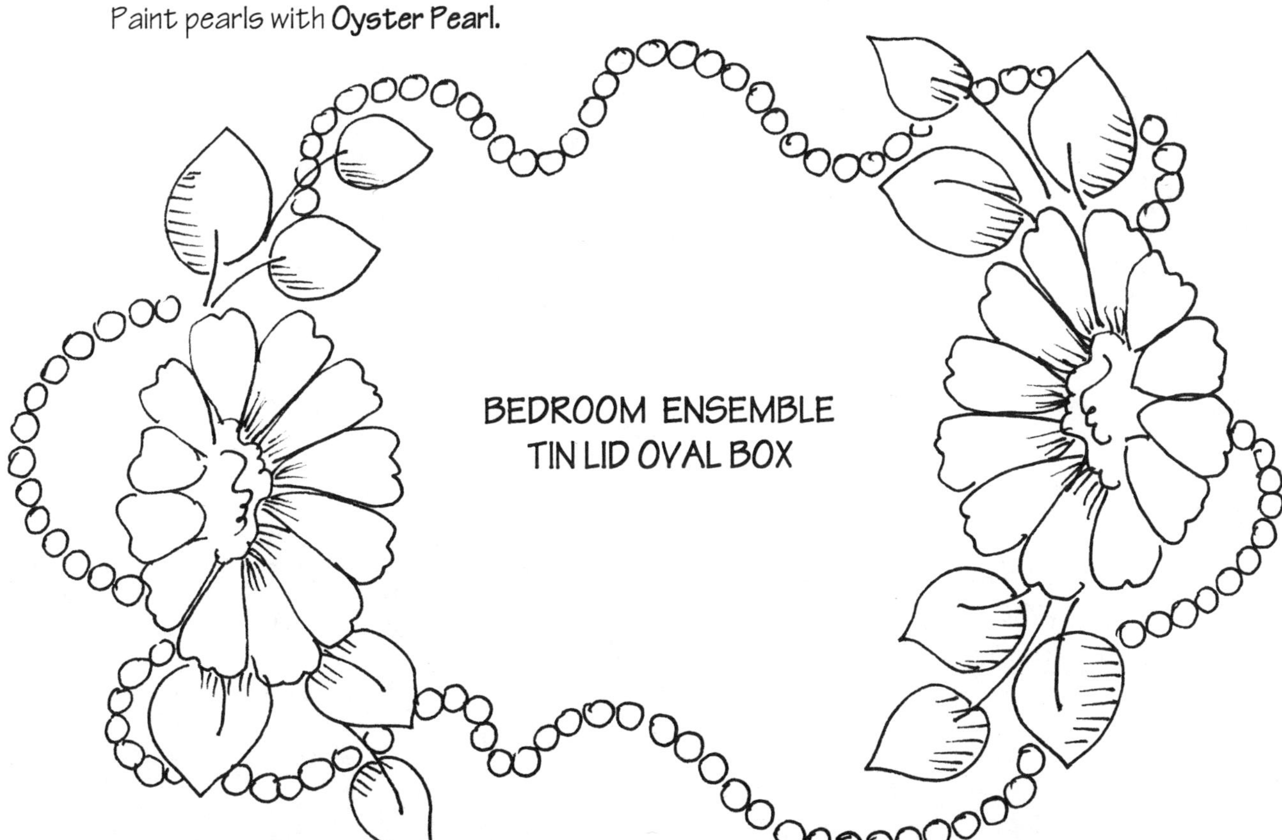

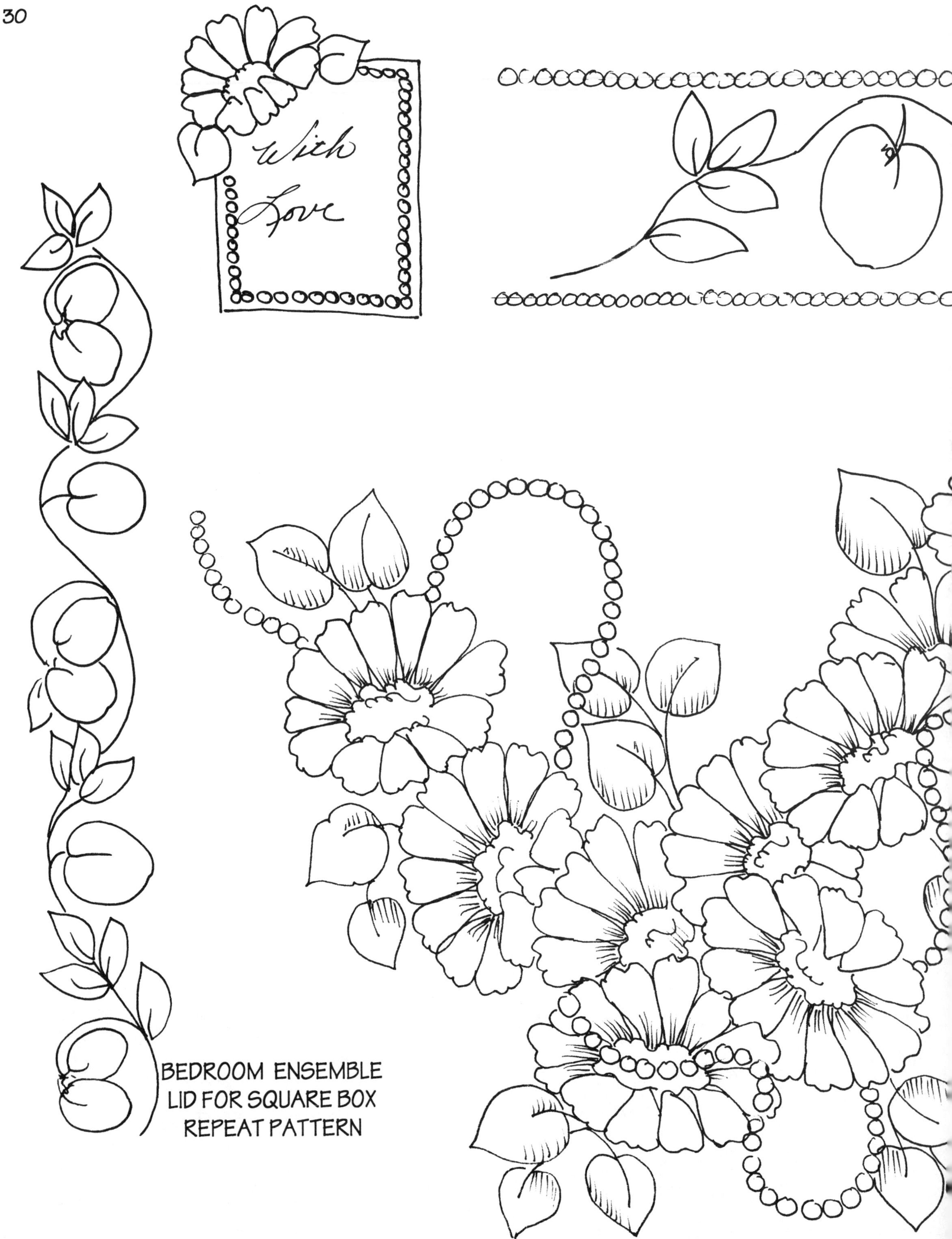

BEDROOM ENSEMBLE
LID FOR SQUARE BOX
REPEAT PATTERN

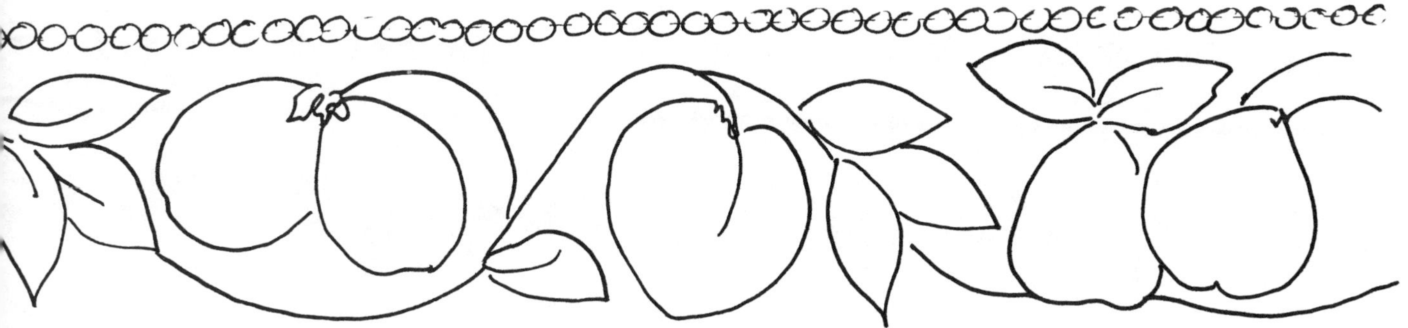

BEDROOM ENSEMBLE
SQUARE BOX
REPEAT PATTERN

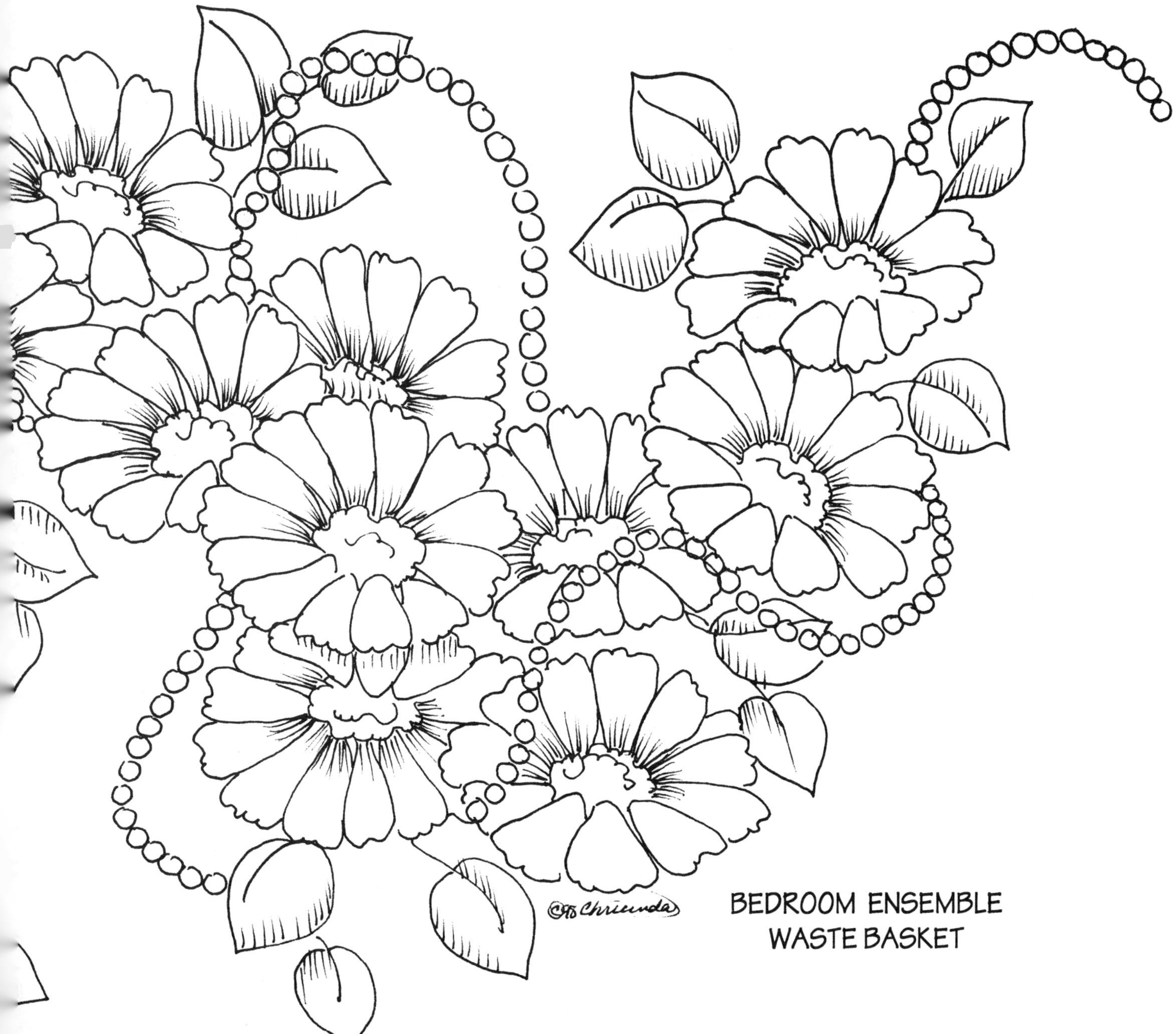

BEDROOM ENSEMBLE
WASTE BASKET

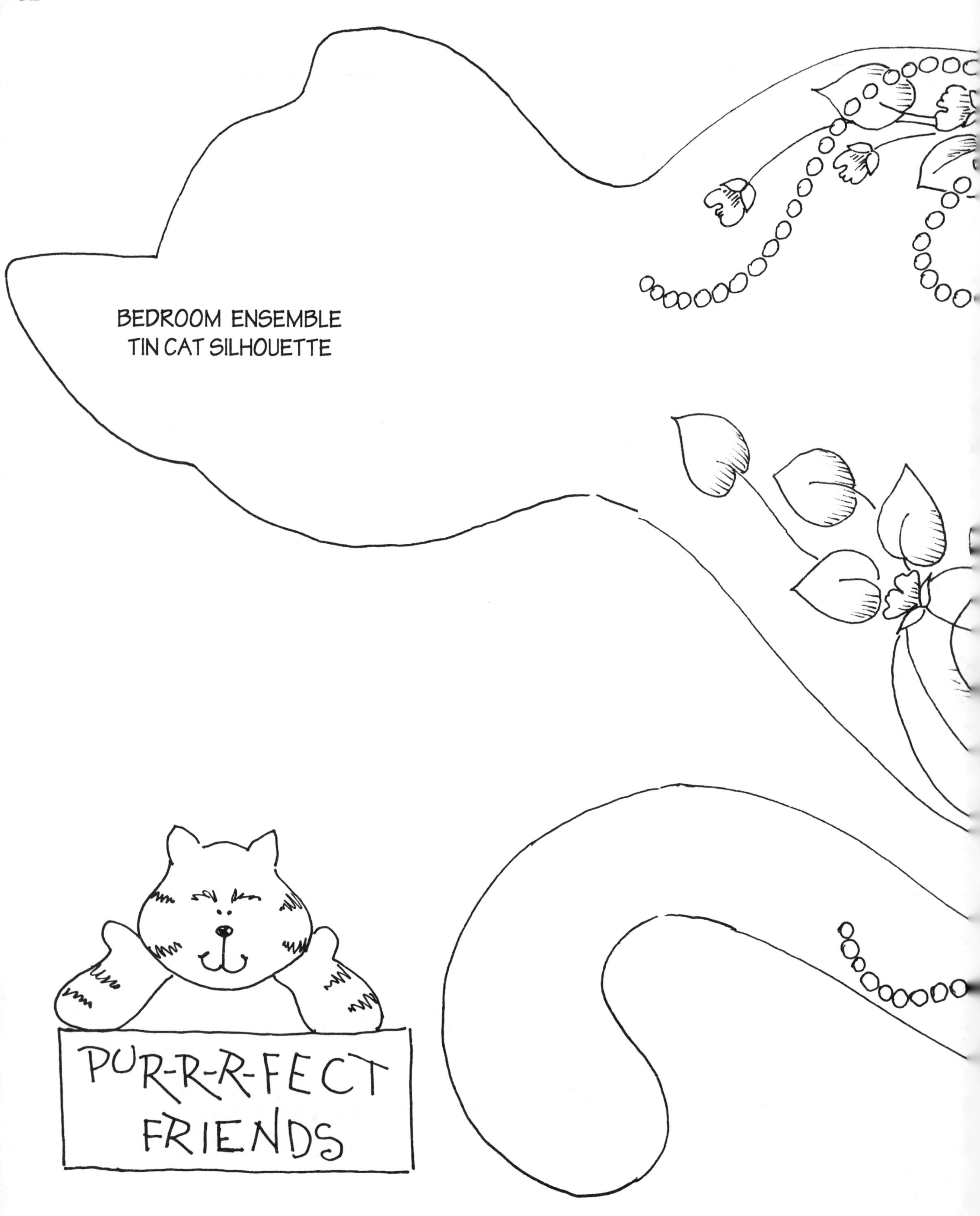
BEDROOM ENSEMBLE
TIN CAT SILHOUETTE
PUR-R-R-FECT
FRIENDS

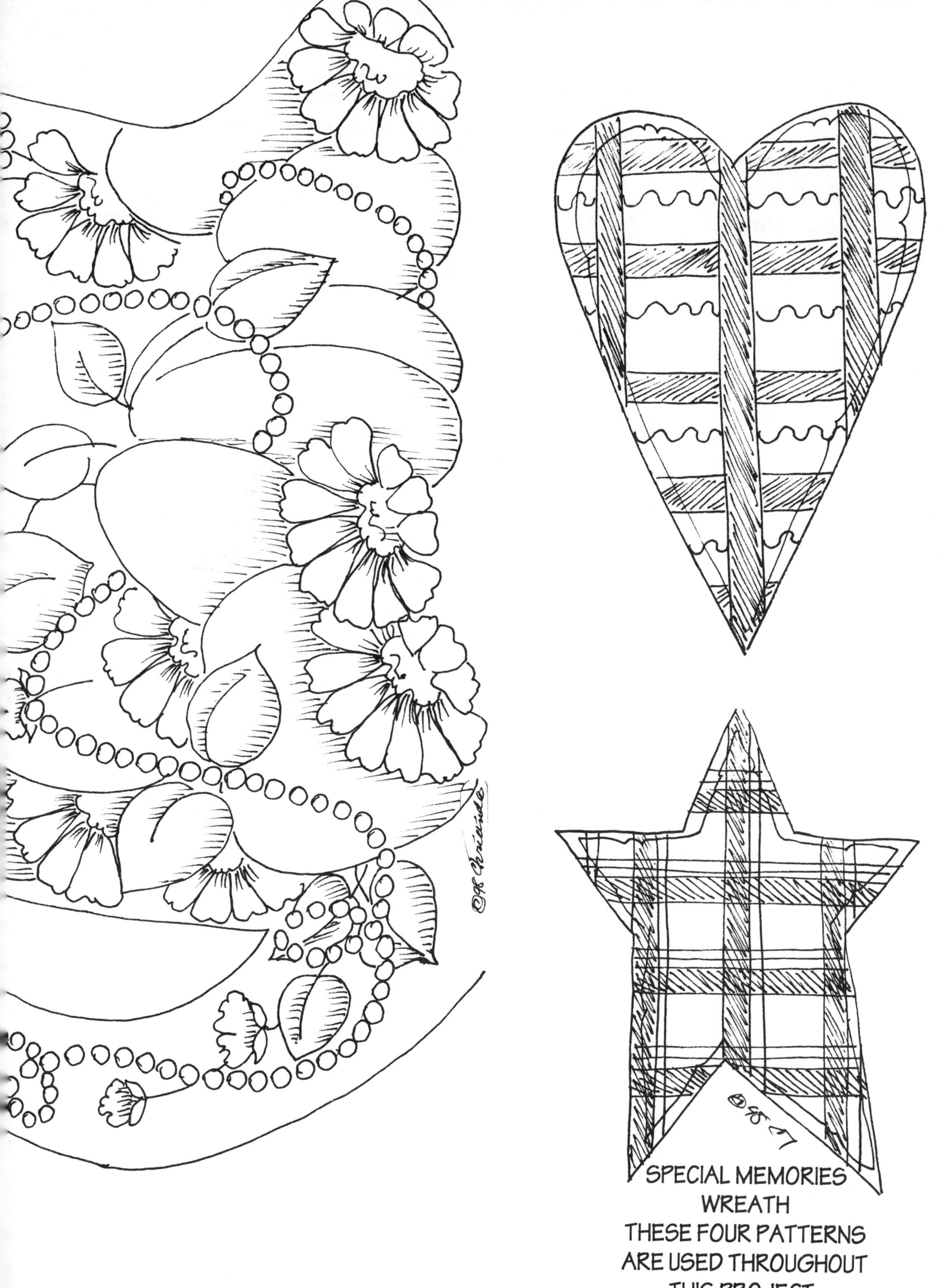

SPECIAL MEMORIES
WREATH
THESE FOUR PATTERNS
ARE USED THROUGHOUT
THIS PROJECT.

SPECIAL MEMORIES
BOX LIDS
ADJUST PATTERN TO FIT TOP OF EACH LID

GOLDEN STRAW
WHITE
FOREST GREEN
ULTRA DEEP BLUE

SPECIAL MEMORIES WREATH
THESE FOUR PATTERNS
ARE USED THROUGHOUT
THIS PROJECT.

SPECIAL MEMORIES
MEDIUM BOX
REPEAT PATTERN

WHITE

SPECIAL MEMORIES
SMALL BOX
REPEAT PATTERN

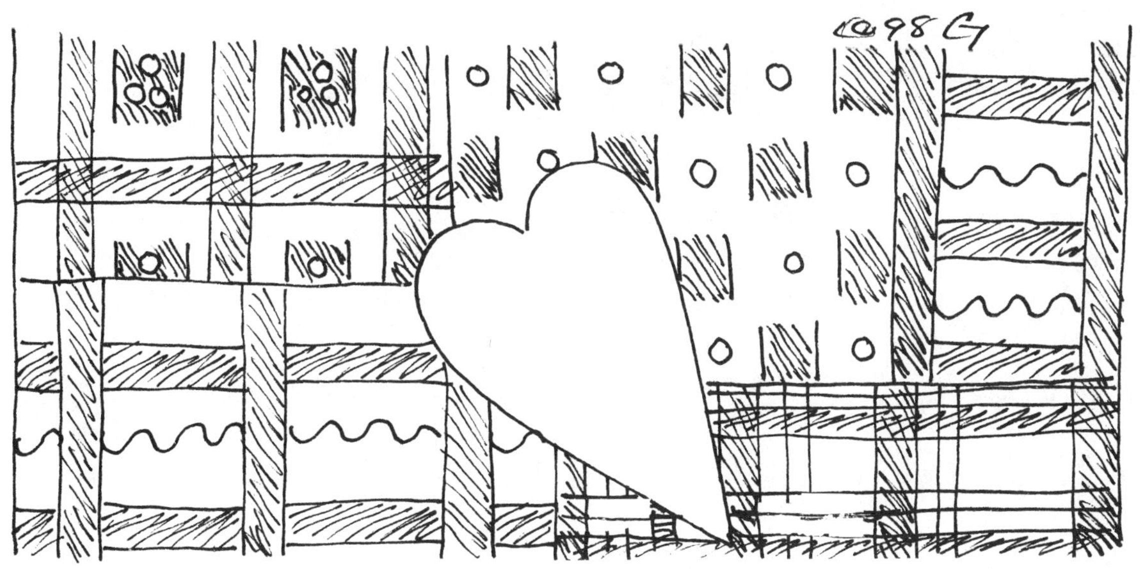

SPECIAL MEMORIES
LARGE BOX
REPEAT PATTERN

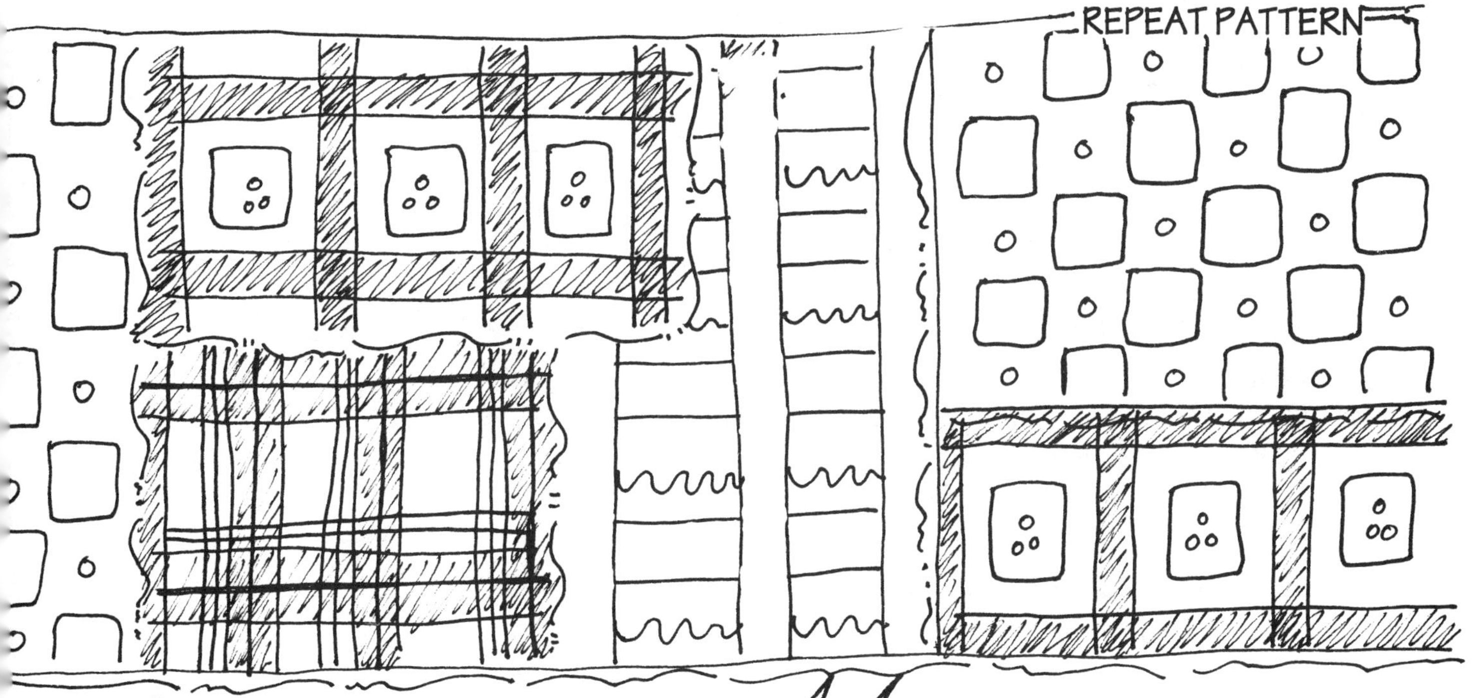

Special Memories

SPECIAL MEMORIES
Boxes, Picture Frame and Tin Wreath

DecoArt Americana Colors:
DA67 Black
DA111 Grey Sky
DA168 Golden Straw
DA112 Cranberry Wine
DA1 White
DA100 Ultra Deep Blue
DA50 Forest Green

DecoArt Patio Paints
DCP10 Summer Sky Blue
DCP21 Wrought Iron Black

DecoArt Specialty Product:
DAS13 Matte Spray
DS17 Multi-Purpose Sealer

Misc. Supplies:
Glue Gun
Tacky Glue
Blue Paper Twist
Wire
Craft Stick

Painting Instructions all Pieces:
1. Basecoat boxes and picture frame in **Grey Sky.**
2. Apply one coat of **Multi Purpose Sealer** to all tin pieces.
3. Float with **Ultra Deep Blue** the band on frame and large box and hearts on small box.

Surfaces by DC&C
Large Sq. Boxes with Rusty Tin Round Corners #28-9254
Tin-Tiques for Boxes:
Four Stars #24-7225
Twelve Stars #24-7223
Four Houses #24-7119
Four Houses #24-7118
Four Chimney Houses #24-7120
Four Hearts #24-7201
Picture Oval Frame Straight Tin Corners #28-9271
Tin-Tiques for Frame:
One House #24-7119
One House #24-7118
Two Hearts #24-7201
Rusty Tin Crazy Wire Wreath #24-7414
Tin-Tiques for Wreath:
Two Folk Hearts #24-7201 One #24-7205, One #24-7207
Two Stars #24-7223
One House #24-7123, Two Houses #24-7119
One Birdhouse #24-7126, One Birdhouse #24-7125
One Folk Art Bird #24-7127
One Tree #24-7135
Natural Jute Wired Ribbon #35-6501

SPECIAL MEMORIES BOXES, PICTURE FRAME AND TIN WREATH **Continued**

Patchwork as follows this includes tin pieces on wreath:
1. Blue: Stripe with **Ultra Deep Blue**, check **Cranberry Wine**, dots **White.**
   Yellow plaid: Do **Golden Straw, Ultra Deep Blue**, and **Forest Green** horizontal and then vertical. Do horizontal and vertical **White.** Green: Check **Forest Green**, dot **White.**
   Burgundy: Stripe **Cranberry Wine, Golden Straw**, wiggly line **White.**
2. Float around all of the patches with **Grey Sky** plus a touch of **Black.**
3. Do all lettering and liner-work with **Black.**

To Finish all pieces:
1. Spray all pieces including tin with **Matte Spray.**
2. Antique with a mix of **Summer Sky Blue** plus a touch of **Wrought Iron Black.**
3. Glue all ribbon in place, and then Tin-tiques. On tiny Tin-tiques glued to larger ones on wreath I placed a piece of craft stick in between the two pieces to give depth.

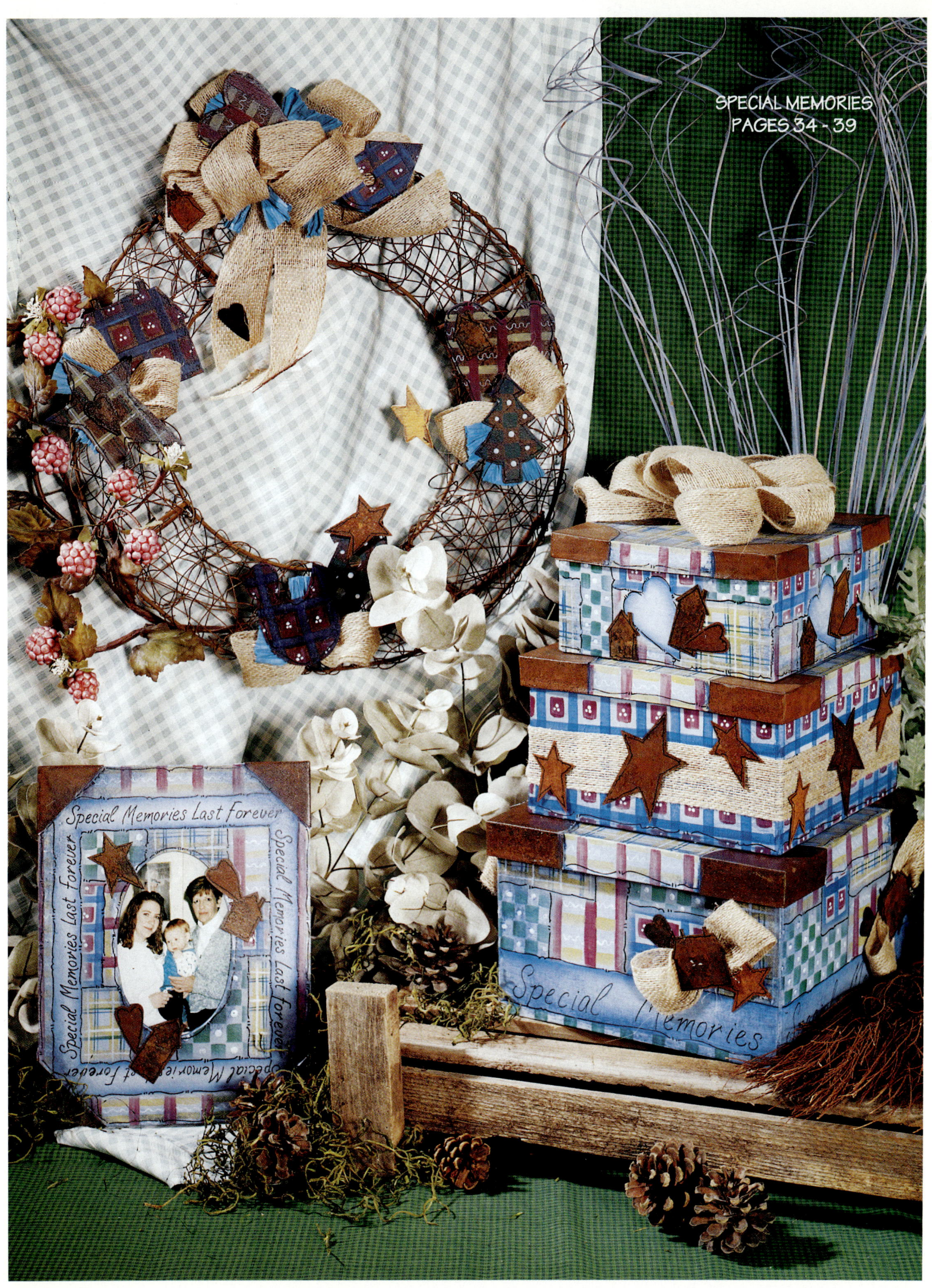

SPECIAL MEMORIES
PAGES 34 - 39

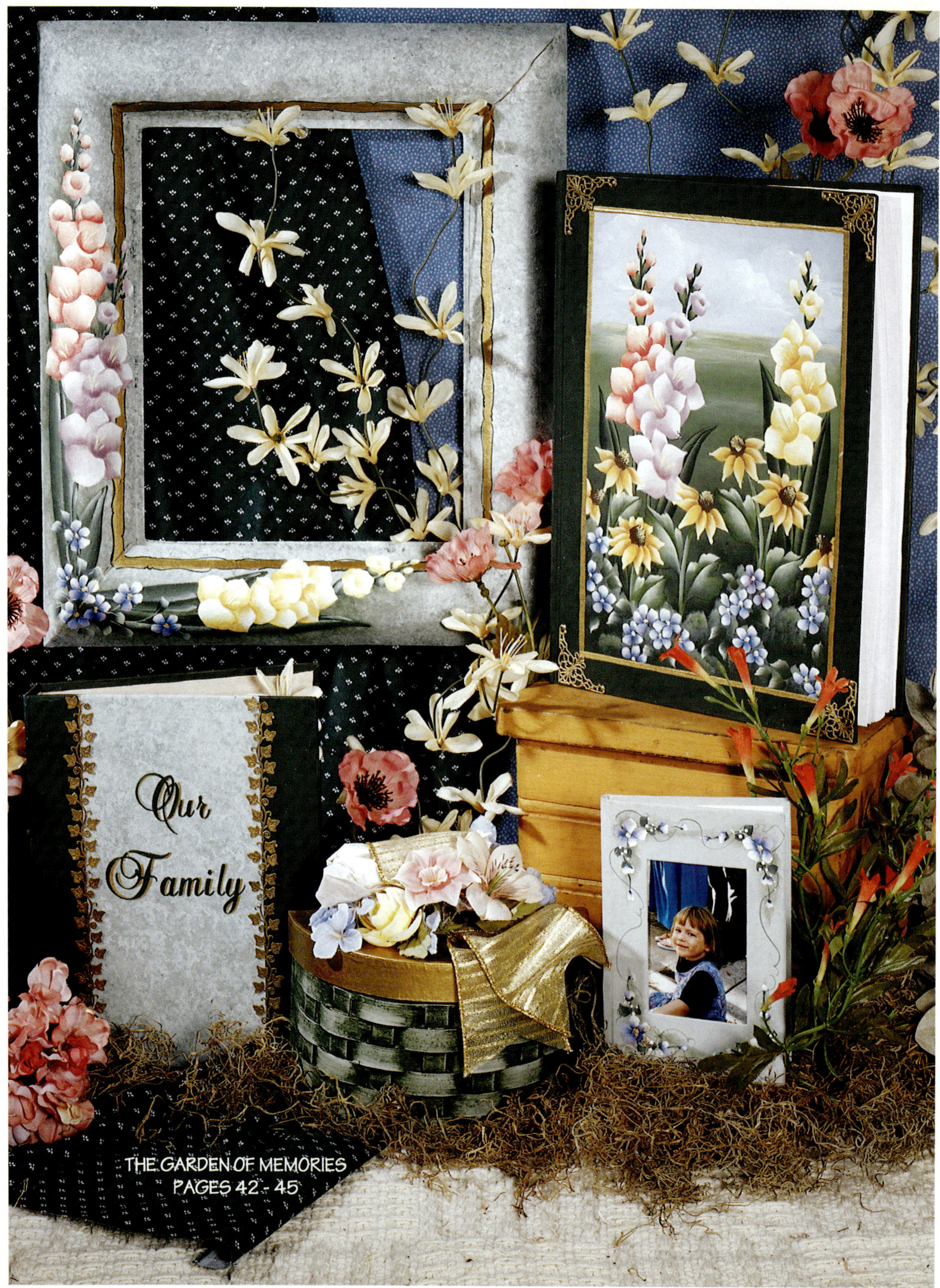

THE GARDEN OF MEMORIES
PAGES 42 - 45

SPECIAL MEMORIES
FRAME

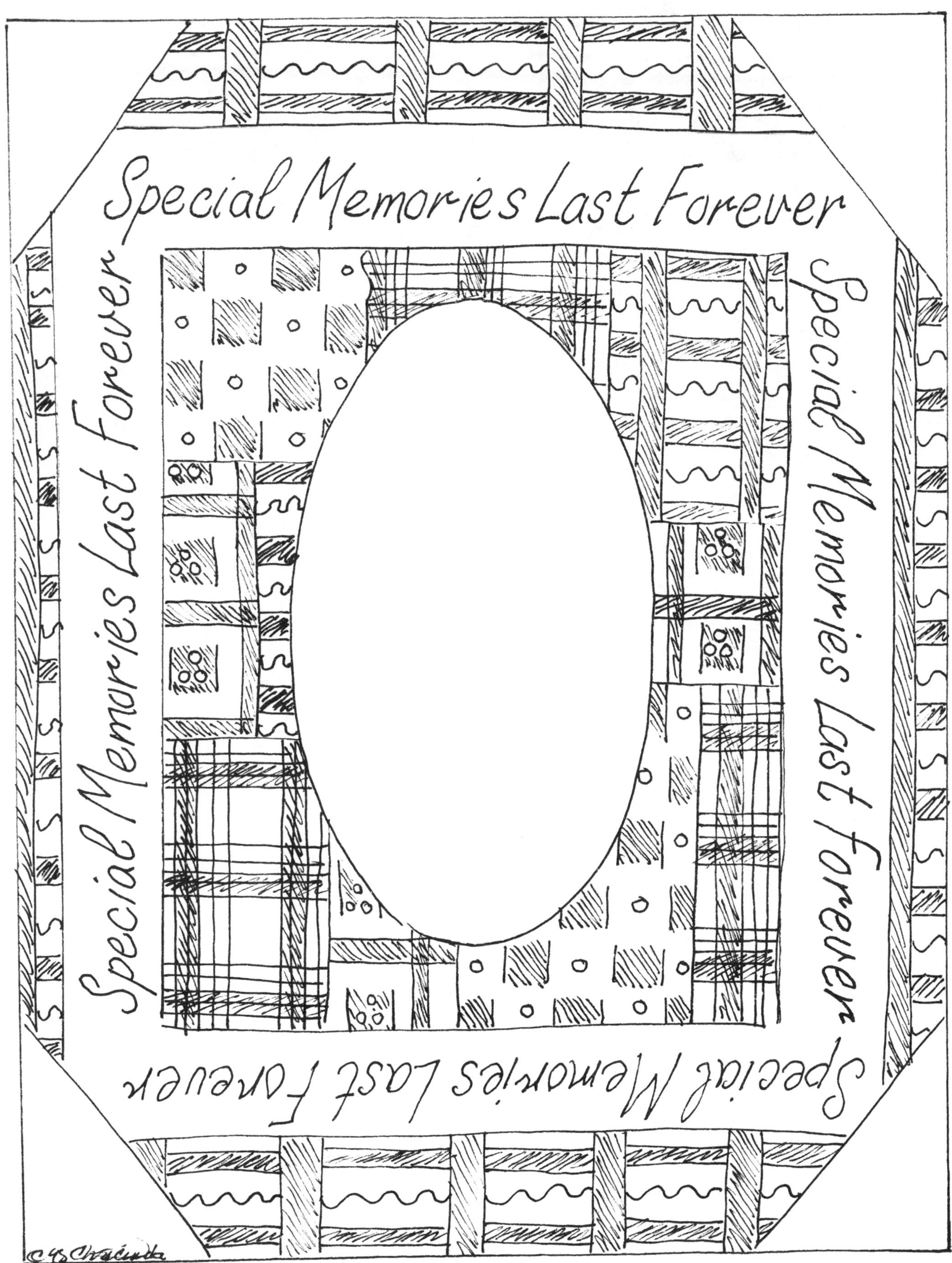

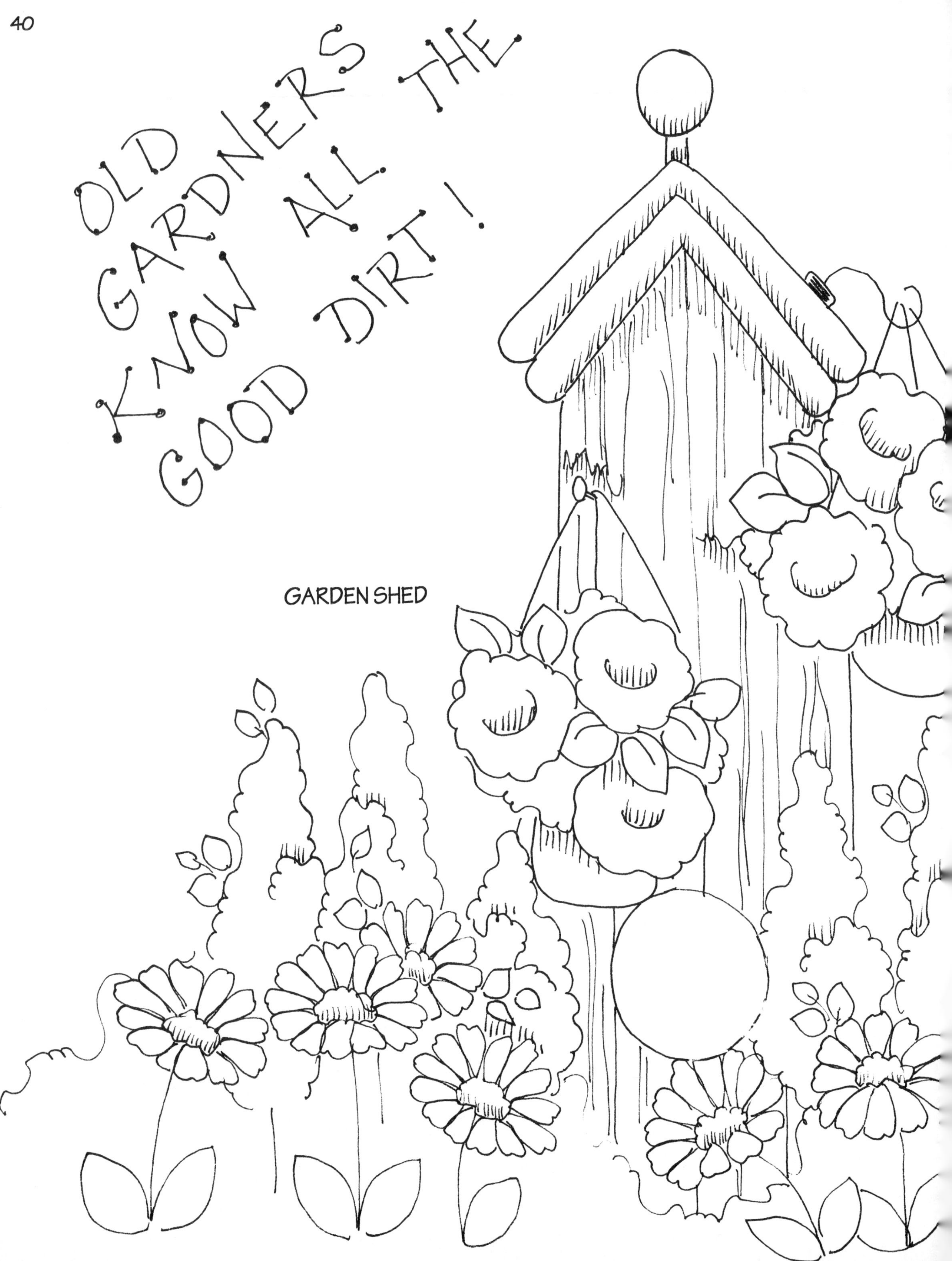

GARDEN SHED

GARDEN SHED

DecoArt Americana Colors

DA153 Eggshell
DA64 Burnt Umber
DA82 Evergreen
DA141 Blue Violet
DA131 Hauser Light Green
DA99 Sapphire Blue
DA176 Olde Gold
DA67 Black
DA150 Royal Purple
DA1 White
DA79 Brandy Wine
DA41 Country Blue
DA27 Gooseberry Pink

DecoArt Patio Paint:

DCP18 Woodland Brown

DecoArt Specialty Products:

DAS8 Weathered Wood
DS18 Multi-Purpose Sealer

Surface by DC&C

Pot Bellies Gourd #28-0202
Garden Tools #52-0100
Tin-tiques sign #24-7110

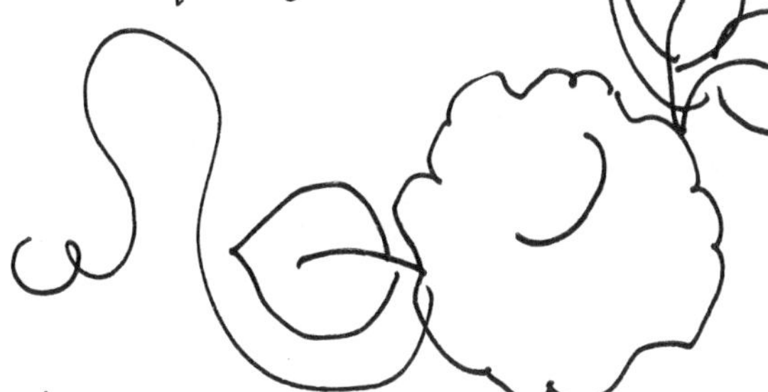

Miscellaneous Supplies:

Glue Gun
Twine

Painting Instructions:

1. Apply one even coat of **Multi Purpose Sealer** to tin piece.
2. With a wet in wet technique apply **White** and **Sapphire Blue** to the sky area, using more **White** then **Sapphire.**
3. Basecoat the entire birdhouse in **Black**. Apply one coat of **Weathered Wood**. Allow to dry thoroughly. Apply one coat of **Eggshell** to the walls, **Brandy Wine** to the roof, and **Olde Gold** to the ball on top.
4. Glaze and float the shadows of the walls **Burnt Umber**.
5. Float the shadows on the roof with **Black.** Float the highlights with **White** plus a touch of **Brandy Wine.**
6. Float the shadows on the ball with **Burnt Umber**, float the highlights with **White** plus a touch of **Olde Gold.**
7. Do the baskets in **Olde Golde** plus a touch of **Burnt Umber**. Float the highlights with **White** plus a touch of **Olde Golde.**
8. Stipple the greenery in **Evergreen** tipped in **Hauser Light Green** and a touch of **Eggshell.**
9. Basecoat the **Gooseberry Pink** flowers, float the shadows with **Brandy Wine.** Float the highlights with **White** plus a touch of Gooseberry Pink.
10. Stipple tall flowers in **Blue Violet** plus a touch of **Royal Purple** tipped in **White.**
11. Stroke the daisies in **White.** Stipple the centers in **Old Golde** and **Burnt Umber**. Stroke all leaves in **Evergreen.**
12. Do stem in **Burnt Umber.**

To Finish: Spray with **Matte Spray.** Antique with **Woodland Brown.** Attach pieces.

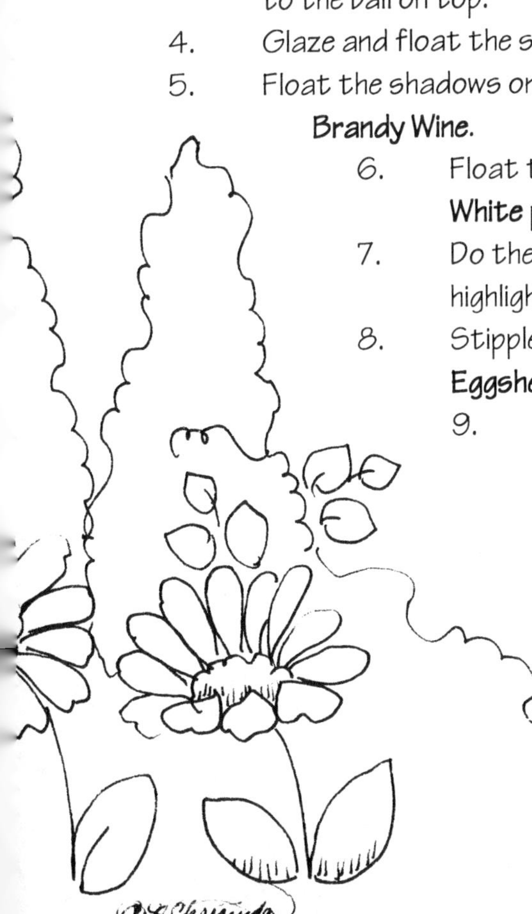

THE GARDEN OF MEMORIES

DecoArt Americana Colors:

DA1 White
DA106 Lt. Avocado
DA23 Peaches N Cream
DA150 Royal Purple
DA157 Black Green
DA71 Glorious Gold
DA168 Golden Straw
DA6 Pineapple
DA156 Antique Rose
DA41 Country Blue
DA65 Dark Chocolate
DA149 Silver Sage Green
DA185 Light French Blue
DA163 Honey Brown
DA109 Taupe
DA141 Blue Violet
DA82 Evergreen

DecoArt Specialty Product:

DS18 Faux Glaze Medium

Surfaces by DC&C

Memory Album/Journal #22-2501
Address Book #22-2504
Woven Box #28-4112
Small Ivy Border #24-7232
Ribbon Gold Iridescent w/Gold Stripes #35-6256
Photo Album #22-2506
Picture Frame #28-4032
4 Embossed Corners #24-7263

Miscellaneous Supplies:

Seawool Sponge
Tacky Glue
Hot Glue Gun
Flowers

Painting Instructions for Journal:

1. Basecoat the sky in **Lt. French Blue.** While still wet streak with **White.**
2. Basecoat the ground in **Lt. Avocado,** while still wet streak with **Evergreen** and **Golden Straw,** with a little **White** along the sky line. Float shadows behind flowers with **Black Green.**
3. Basecoat the glad leaves in **Black Green,** float the highlights with **Lt. Avocado.**
4. Glads area as follows: Basecoat **Peaches N Cream** plus a touch of **White,** float the shadows with **Antique Rose.** Float the highlights with **White** plus a touch of **Peaches N Cream.** Basecoat **Taupe** plus a touch of **White.** Float the shadows lightly with **Royal Purple** plus a touch of **Dk. Chocolate,** float the highlights with **White** plus a touch of **Taupe.** Basecoat in **Pineapple,** float the shadow with **Golden Straw** and the highlights with **White** plus a touch of **Pineapple.**
5. Basecoat the black-eyed susan leaves in a mix of equal parts **Evergreen** and **Lt. Avocado.** Float the shadows with **Evergreen** and the highlights with **Lt. Avocado** plus a touch of **Pineapple.**
6. Basecoat the black-eyed susans in **Golden Straw.** Float the shadows with **Honey Brown,** and the highlights with **Pineapple.**

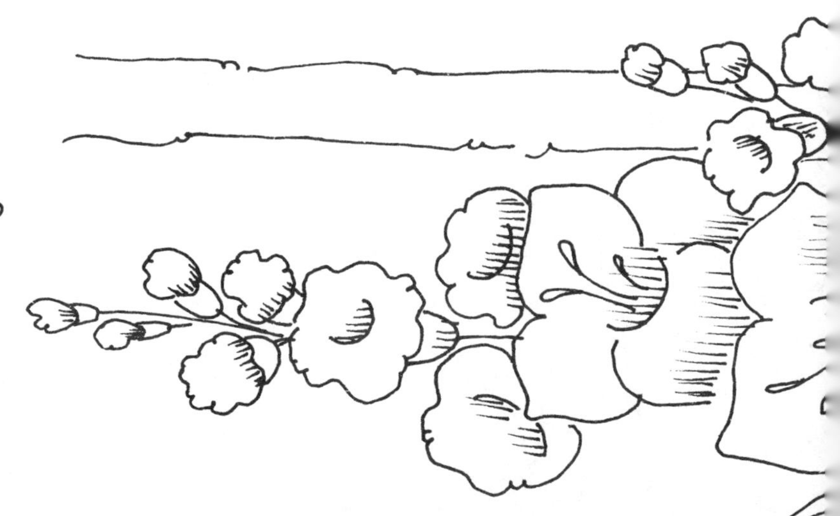

Continued THE GARDEN OF MEMORIES

Basecoat the centers in **Dk. Chocolate**, stipple with **Pineapple**.

7. Basecoat the bottom bush sections in **Evergreen**. Highlight with **Silver Sage Green**.
8. Basecoat the small flowers in a mix of equal parts **Country Blue** and **White**. Float the shadows with **Blue Violet** and the highlights in **White** plus a touch of one of the following **Pineapple**, **Peaches N Cream** or **Taupe**. Stroke the small leaves in **Black Green** tipped in **Pineapple**.
9. Basecoat the edge in **Evergreen** and band with **Glorious Gold**. Dry-brush the tin embossed corners with **Glorious Gold** and glue in place.

Address Book:

1. Basecoat in **Silver Sage Green**. Float **Evergreen** behind the pattern area.
2. Do the small flowers and the leaves according to step #8 of the Journal. Do the accent dots in **Peaches N Cream** plus a touch of **White**.

Photo Album:

1. With seawool sponge apply **Silver Sage Green** and a touch of **Evergreen** to the center section.
2. Basecoat the edges and the lettering in **Evergreen**.
3. Dry-brush the ivy border with **Glorious Gold**. Line lettering **Glorious Gold**. Glue border in place.

Frame:

1. With seawool sponge apply **Silver Sage Green** with a touch of **Evergreen**. Do the banding in **Glorious Gold** lined with **Evergreen**.
2. Basecoat the glad leaves in **Lt. Avocado** plus a touch of **Evergreen**, float the shadows with **Evergreen** and the highlights with **Pineapple** plus a touch of **Lt. Avocado**.
3. Do the glads according to Step #4 of the Journal and the small flowers according to Step #8.

THE GARDEN OF MEMORIES
PICTURE FRAME

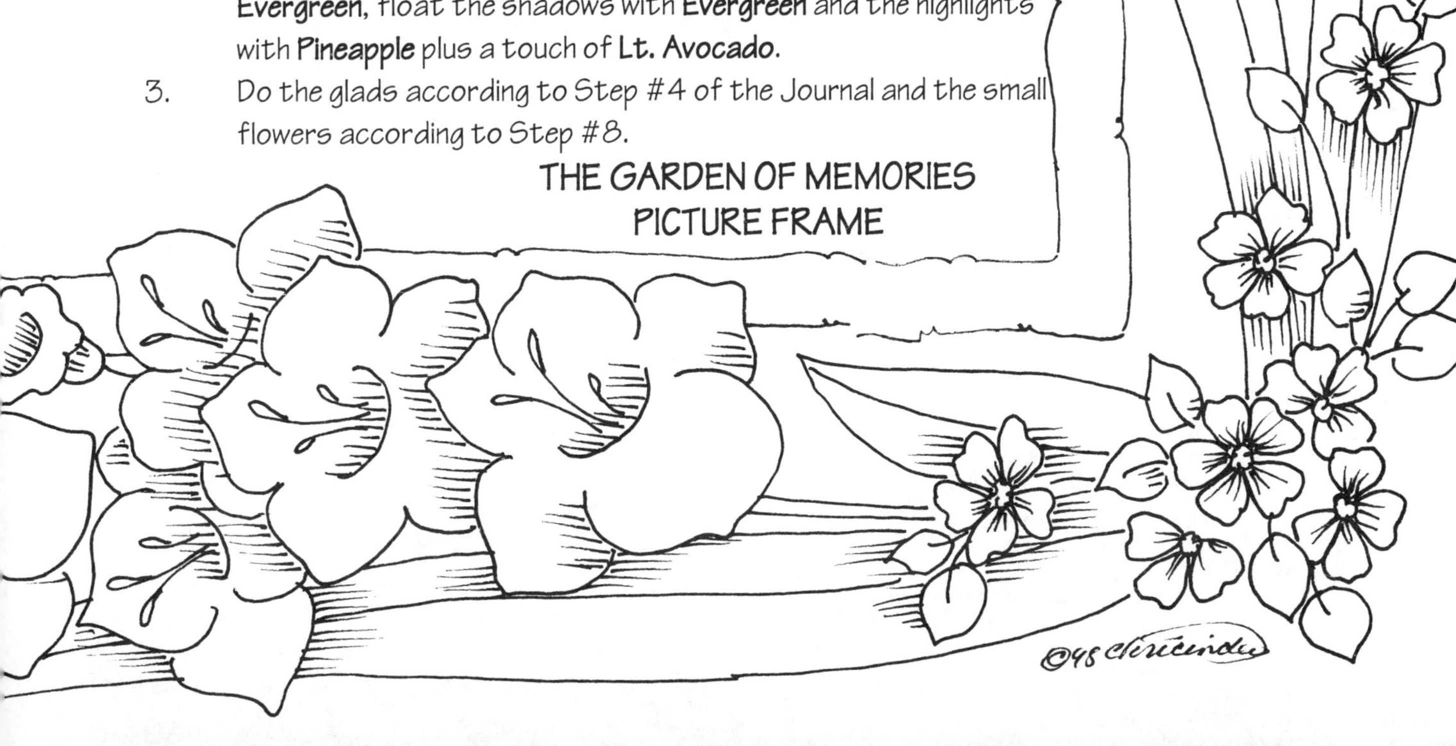

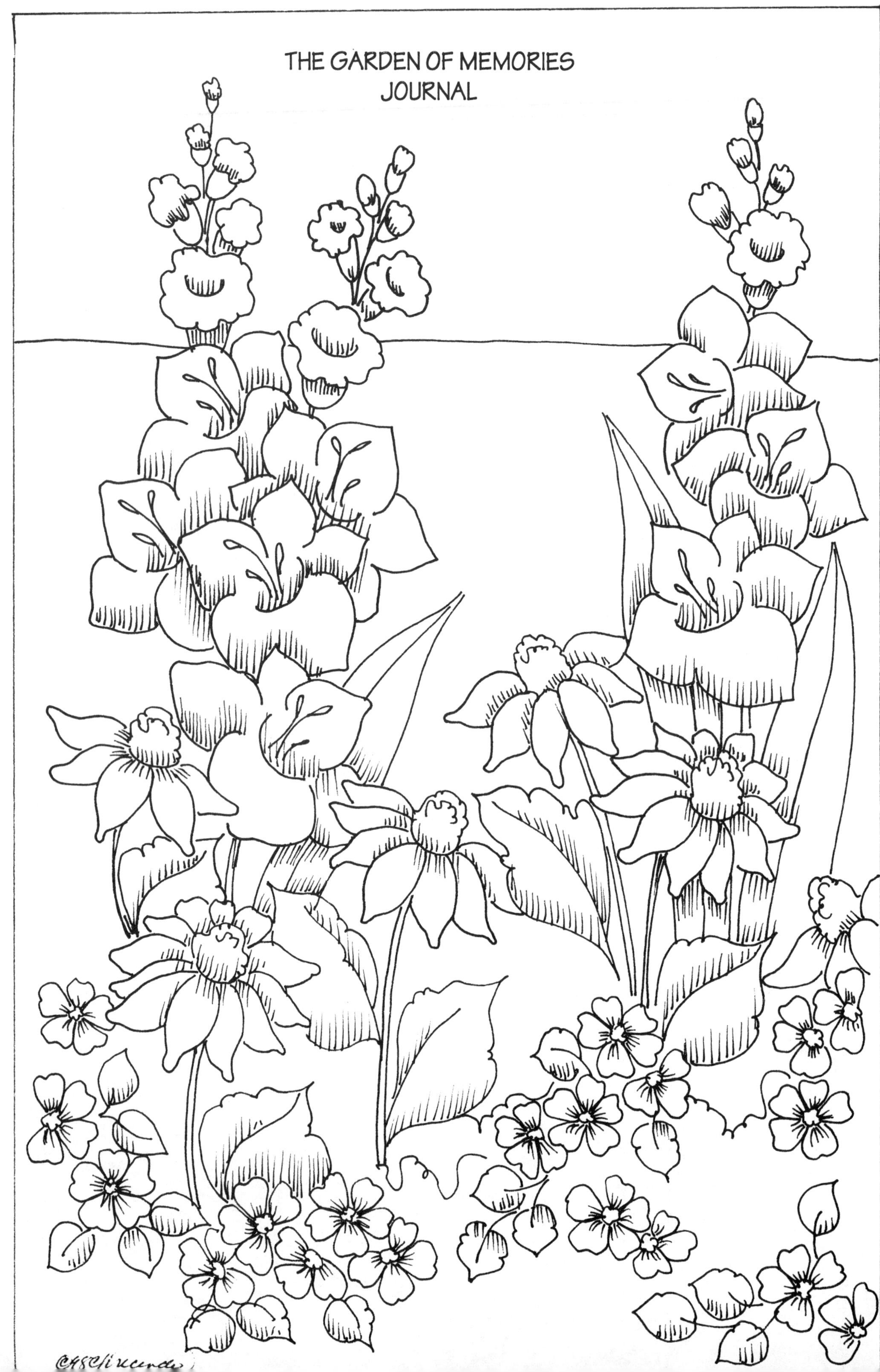
THE GARDEN OF MEMORIES
JOURNAL

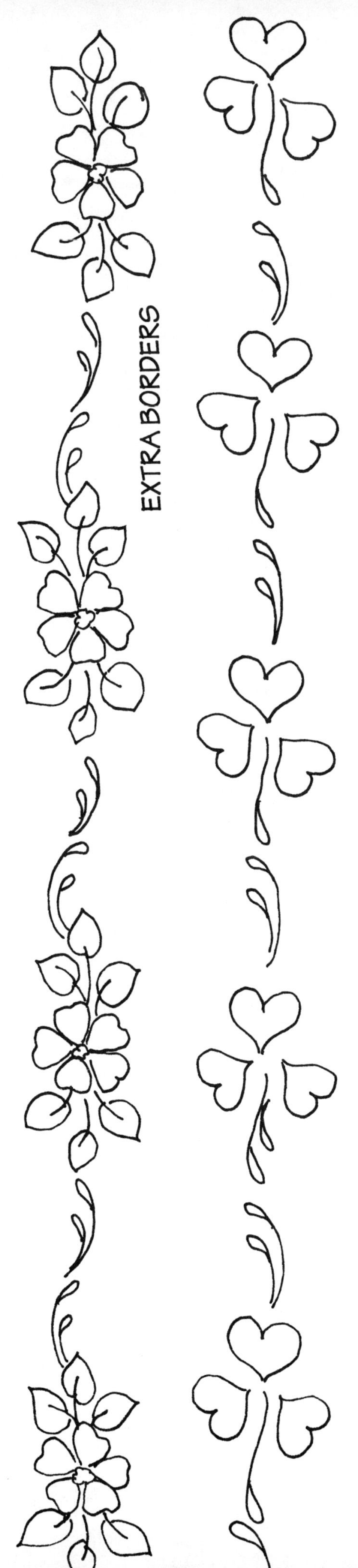

Continued THE GARDEN OF MEMORIES

Woven Box:

1. Basecoat the woven part in **Silver Sage Green**. Antique with a mix of 1 part **Faux Glaze Medium** to 1 part **Evergreen.**
2. Basecoat the lid in **Glorious Gold**.
3. Arrange flowers and ribbon according to color picture.

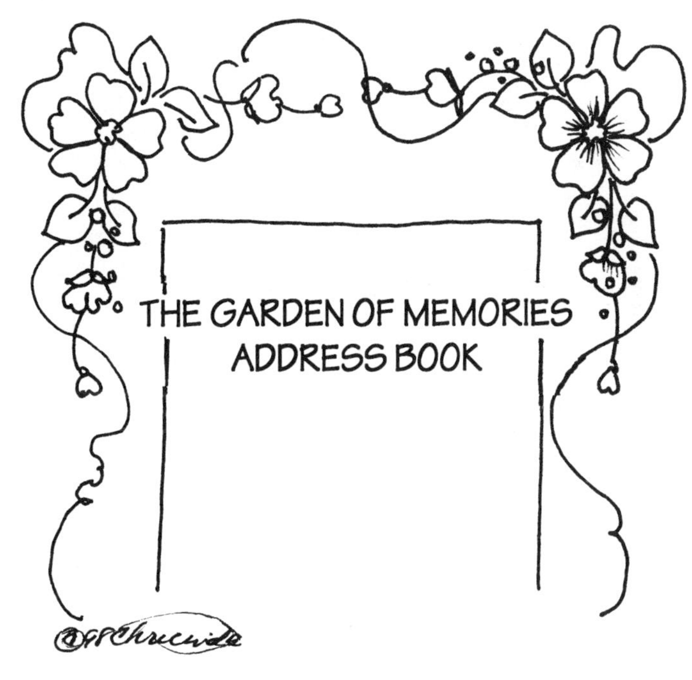

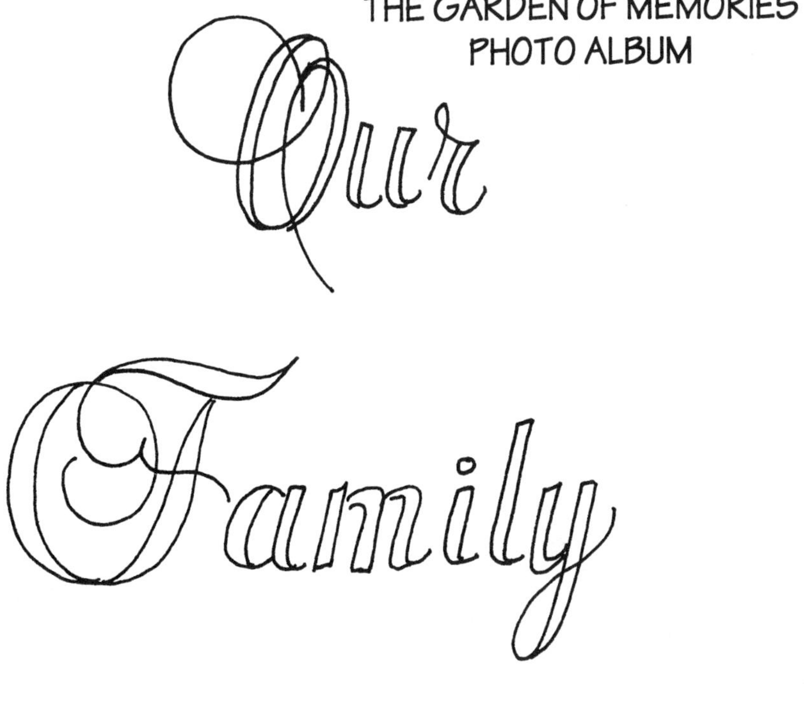

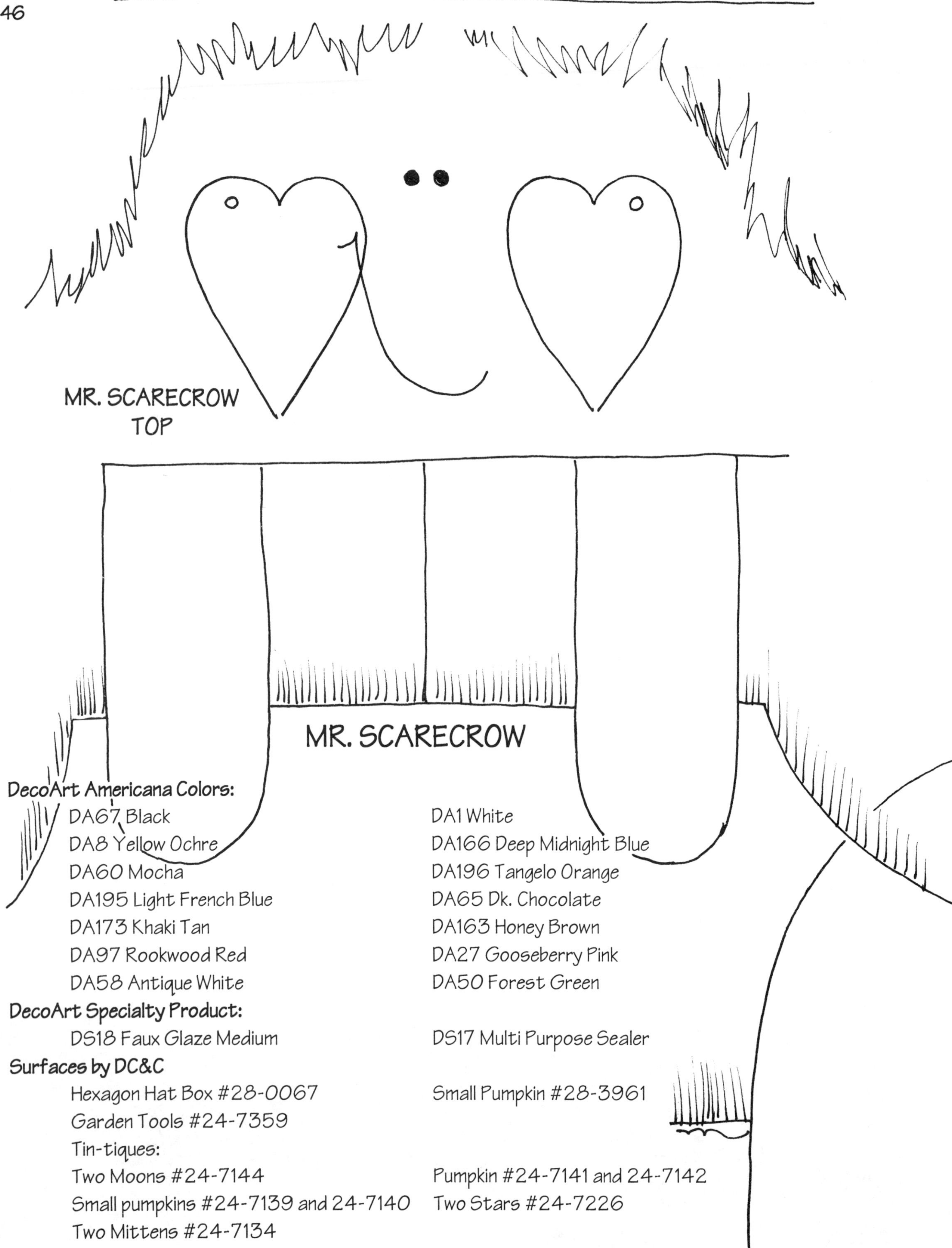

DecoArt Americana Colors:

DA67 Black
DA8 Yellow Ochre
DA60 Mocha
DA195 Light French Blue
DA173 Khaki Tan
DA97 Rookwood Red
DA58 Antique White
DA1 White
DA166 Deep Midnight Blue
DA196 Tangelo Orange
DA65 Dk. Chocolate
DA163 Honey Brown
DA27 Gooseberry Pink
DA50 Forest Green

DecoArt Specialty Product:

DS18 Faux Glaze Medium
DS17 Multi Purpose Sealer

Surfaces by DC&C

Hexagon Hat Box #28-0067
Small Pumpkin #28-3961
Garden Tools #24-7359
Tin-tiques:
Two Moons #24-7144
Pumpkin #24-7141 and 24-7142
Small pumpkins #24-7139 and 24-7140
Two Stars #24-7226
Two Mittens #24-7134

Miscellaneous Supplies:

Raffia	Glue Gun	Fabric	Buttons
Sunflowers	Grapes	Wire	Tacky Glue

Coat all pieces of rusty tin with one even coat of **Multi Purpose Sealer**.

Painting Instructions:

1. Apply one even coat of **Multi Purpose Sealer** to all tin pieces.
2. Basecoat all of the pant areas in **Light French Blue**. With a mix of 2 parts **Faux Glaze Medium** to 1 part **Deep Midnight Blue**. Working one section at a time cover with one even coat of glaze mix, lay a piece of plastic wrap in the wet glaze and lift. Float the shadows with **Deep Midnight Blue** and the highlights with **Light French Blue**.
3. Basecoat his shirt in **Antique White**, float the shadows with **Khaki Tan** and the highlights with **White**.
4. Basecoat his shoes in **Dk. Chocolate**, float the highlights with **Yellow Ochre**.
5. Cut a small jagged hole in one corner of hat with ex-acto blade for raffia to come through. Basecoat the hat pieces in **Yellow Ochre**. With a mix of 2 parts **Faux Glaze Medium** to 1 part **Honey Brown**. Working one section at a time cover with one even coat of glaze mix, lay a piece of plastic wrap in the wet glaze and lift. Basecoat hat band in **Rookwood Red**.
6. Basecoat his face in **Mocha**. Basecoat under the raffia for hair with **Honey Brown**. Float the heart cheeks with **Gooseberry Pink**.
7. Basecoat the small pumpkin in **Tangelo Orange**, dry-brush the highlights **Yellow Ochre**. Antique with a mix of 2 parts **Faux Glaze Medium** to 1 part **Rookwood Red**. Basecoat the stem in **Forest Green**.

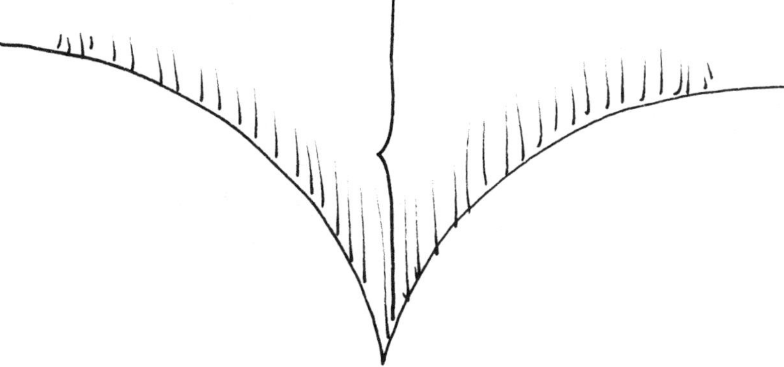

MR. SCARECROW
FEET

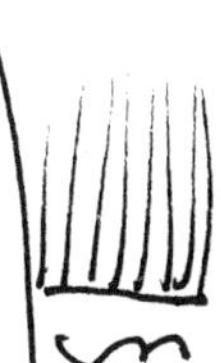

MR. SCARECROW Continued

8. Do all liner work in **Black**.

Tin Pieces:

Dot some with **Tangelo Orange**. Check some with **Yellow Ochre** and run **Black** lines through. Stripe the two small pumpkins that are used as buttons in **Yellow Ochre**. To do plaid on mittens use **Rookwood Red, Antique White**, and **Yellow Ochre.** Do all horizontal and then all vertical.

To Finish:

Tear two pieces of fabric 7 " x 9" glue together along long edge, gather at top and stuff lightly. Punch a hole in the thumb of the mittens. Glue raffia and mittens in place. Run wire through hole in mitten then stem of pumpkin, rake and shovel, and through other mitten. Glue all ties and flowers according to color picture. I have better luck gluing tin pieces in place with tacky glue.

HAPPY PUMPKINS

DecoArt Americana Colors:

DA67 Black
DA196 Tangelo Orange
DA133 Hauser Dark Green
DA1 White
DA97 Rookwood Red
DA150 Royal Purple
DA8 Yellow Ochre
DA50 Forest Green

DecoArt Specialty Product:

DS18 Faux Glaze Medium

Surfaces by DC&C

Witch Hat Pumpkin #28-0370
Happy Pumpkin #28-0371

Miscellaneous Supplies:

Raffia
Sunflowers
Tacky Glue
Sea Wool Sponge
Glue Gun
Wire
Grapes and Fall Leaves

Painting Instructions for both Pumpkins:

1. Basecoat pumpkins in **Tangelo Orange**, dry-brush the highlights **Yellow Ochre.** Antique with a mix of 2 parts **Faux Glaze Medium** to 1 part **Rookwood Red.** Basecoat the stem in **Forest Green.**
2. Basecoat one hat in **Black**. Dry-brush with **Royal Purple.**
3. Basecoat the other hat in **Hauser Dark Green**, on the upper portion of the hat sponge with **Forest Green** and **White.**
4. Do all liner-work in **Black.**

To Finish:

Assemble according to color picture.

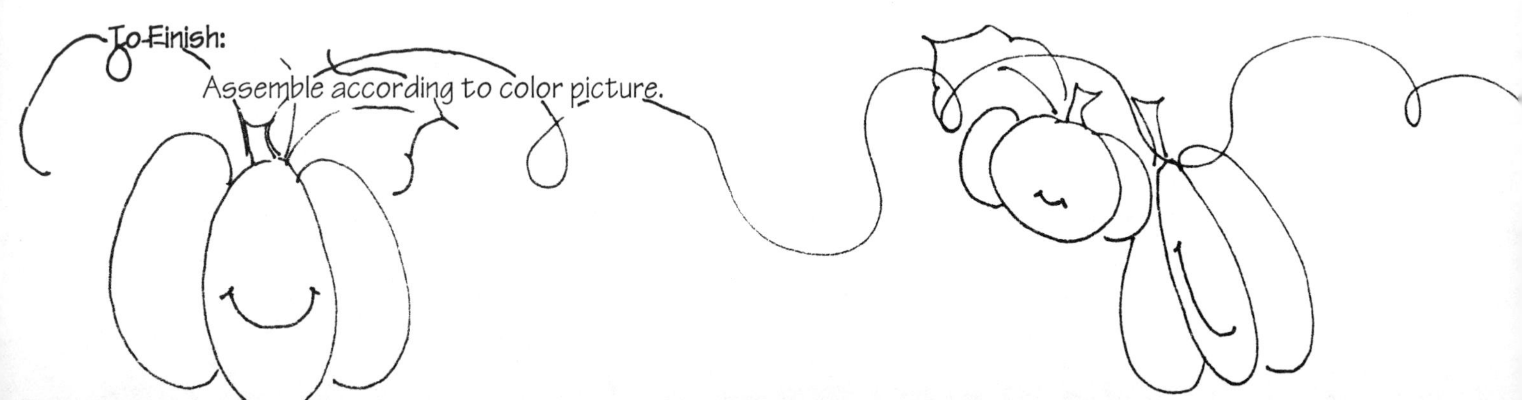

GRANNIE LIVES HERE
KIDS EAT FREE

RUSTY TIN A-FRAME

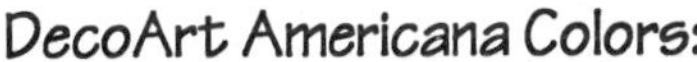

DecoArt Americana Colors:
- DA27 Gooseberry Pink
- DA106 Lt. Avocado
- DA168 Golden Straw
- DA67 Black

DecoArt Patio Paint:
- DCP18 Woodland Brown

DecoArt Specialty Products:
- DS18 Multi Purpose
- DAS13 Matte Spray

Surface by DC&C
- Rusty Tin A-Frame Birdhouse #24-7026

Miscellaneous Supplies:
- Bond 527 Glue
- Buttons all colors and sizes

Painting Instructions:

1. Apply one even coat of **Multi Purpose Sealer** to birdhouse.
2. Do **Gooseberry Pink** stripes on roof, and checks on front of house. Do **Lt. Avocado** checks on front and roof. Do lines **Golden Straw.**
3. Glue buttons with Bond 527. Spatter with Black.
4. Apply an even coat of **Matte Spary.** Antique with **Woodland Brown.**

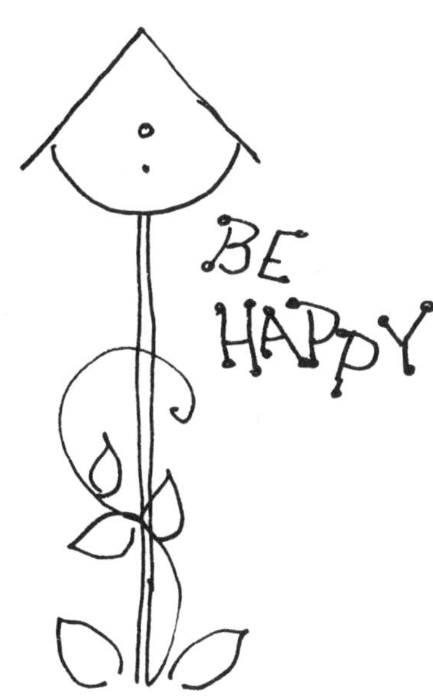

RUSTY TIN A-FRAME
REPEAT PATTERN
FOR ROOF
3/8" CHECKS
ON FRONT

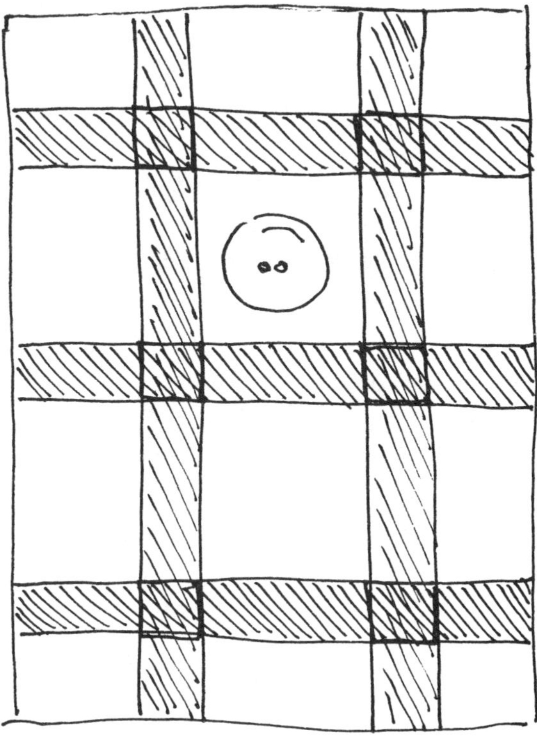

RUSTY CHRISTMAS WREATH

PALETTE - DecoArt Americana Colors:

DA1 White
DA60 Mocha
DA163 Honey Brown
DA18 Country Red
DA27 Gooseberry Pink
DA67 Black
DA158 Antique Teal

DecoArt Patio Paints: DCP18 Woodland Brown

DecoArt Specialty Products:
DAS Snow Tex
DAS13 Matte Spray
DS17 Multi Purpose Sealer

DecoArt Royal Metallics:
DM01 Pale Gold
DM03 Royal Gold

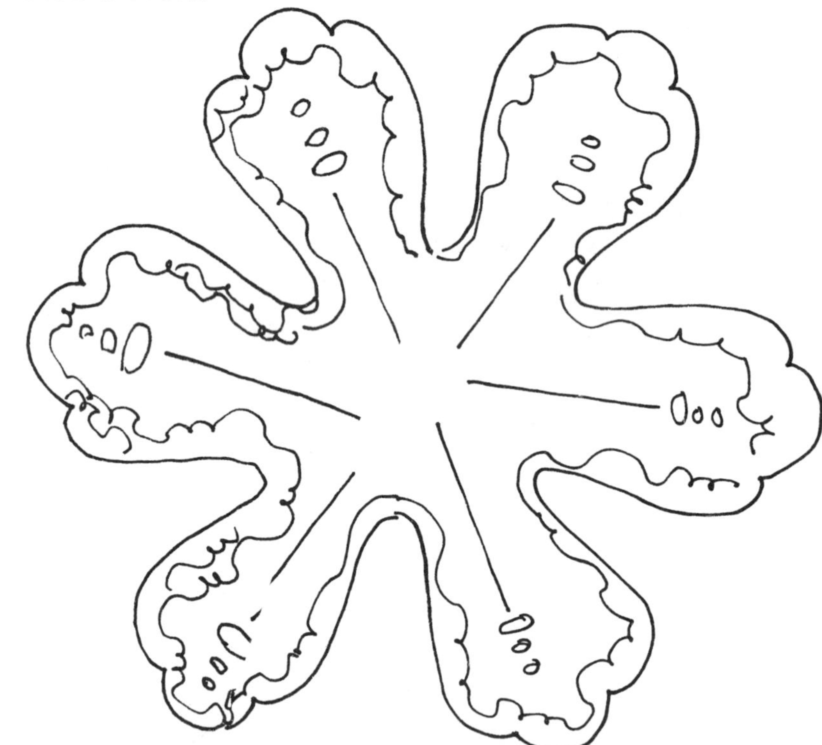

SURFACES by DC&C
Rusty Tin Crazy Wire Wreath #24-7414

Tin-Tiques:
Angel Wings #24-7137
Mitten #24-7134

Rusty Tin Ornaments:
Snowflake #24-7367
Tree #24-7368
Snowman #24-7369
Gingerbread Man #23-7104

MISCELLANEOUS SUPPLIES
Hot Glue Gun
Tacky Glue
Buttons

PAINTING INSTRUCTIONS:

1. Apply one even coat of **Multi Purpose Sealer** to all tin pieces.
2. Stipple the edges of the ornaments, these are the pieces with the attached bows with **Snow Tex.**
3. Stripe the mitten streak the tree and the angel wings all in **Antique Teal** tipped in **White.**
4. Basecoat snowman's hat in **Black.**
5. Do stripes on mittens, hat and streak wings and gingerbread man with **Royal Gold.**
6. Basecoat angel's face in **Mocha,** dry brush cheeks with **Gooseberry Pink.** Basecoat her hair in **Honey Brown** plus a touch of **White.**
7. Do all **Country Red** dot accents.
8. Do all liner work **Black.**
9. Glue on all buttons. Spray with **Matte Spray.** Antique with **Woodland Brown.** Drybrush highlights of **Pale Gold** on all pieces.

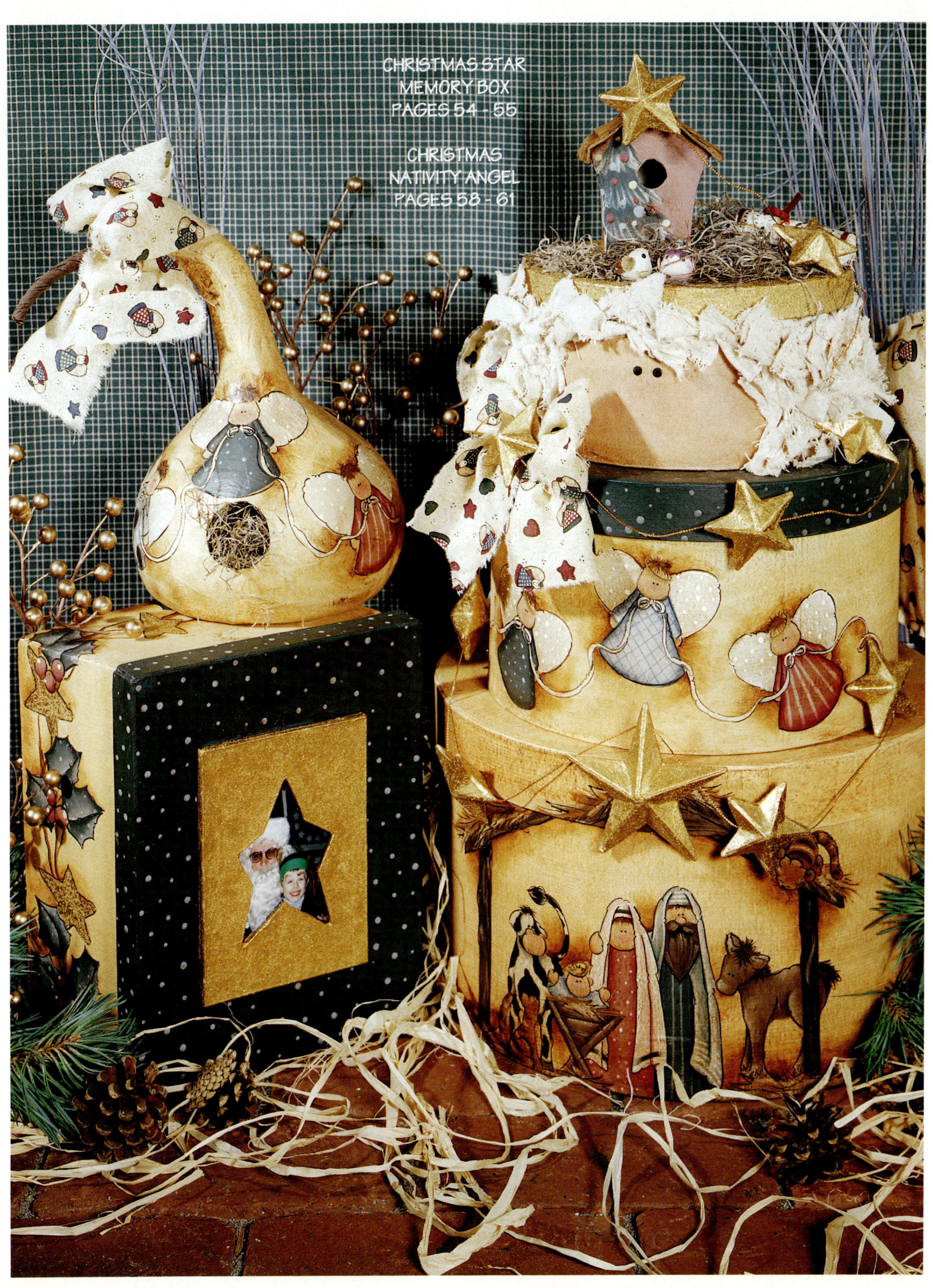
CHRISTMAS STAR
MEMORY BOX
PAGES 54 - 55

CHRISTMAS
NATIVITY ANGEL
PAGES 58 - 61

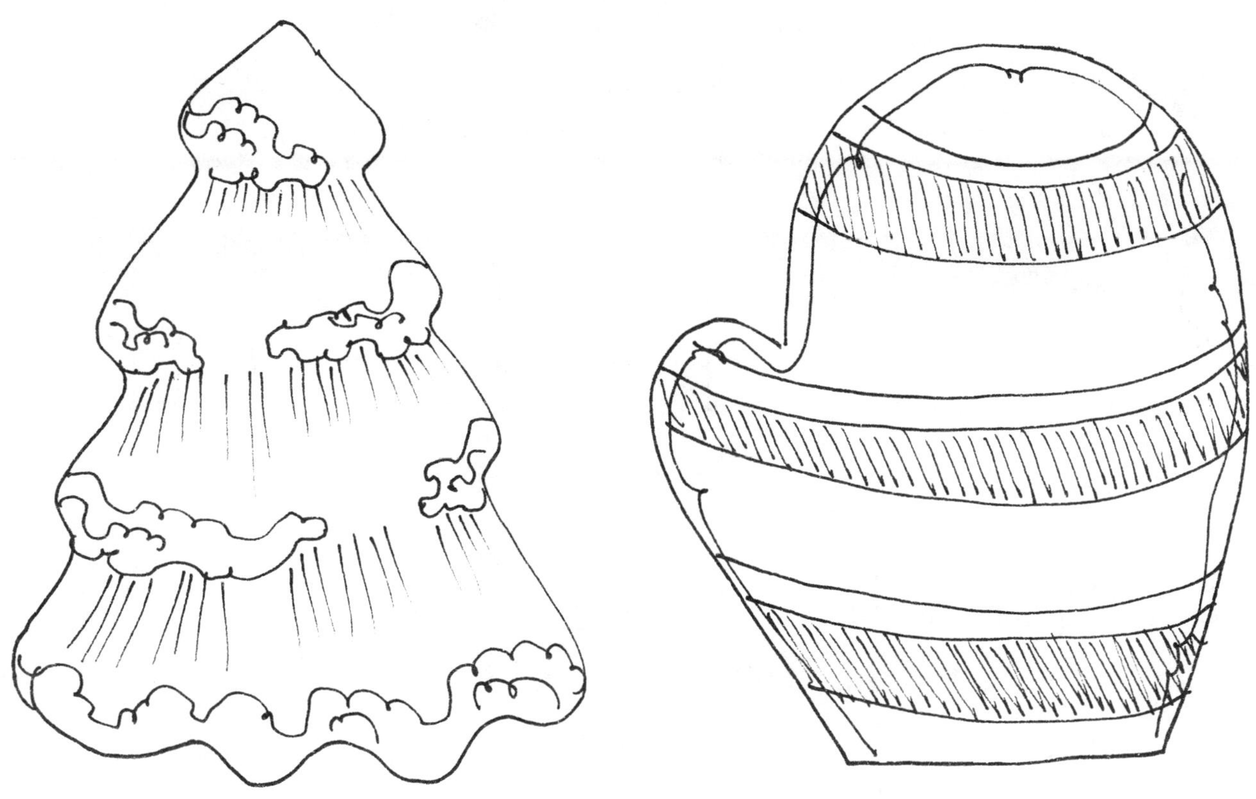

HEARTS
COME HOME FOR
CHRISTMAS

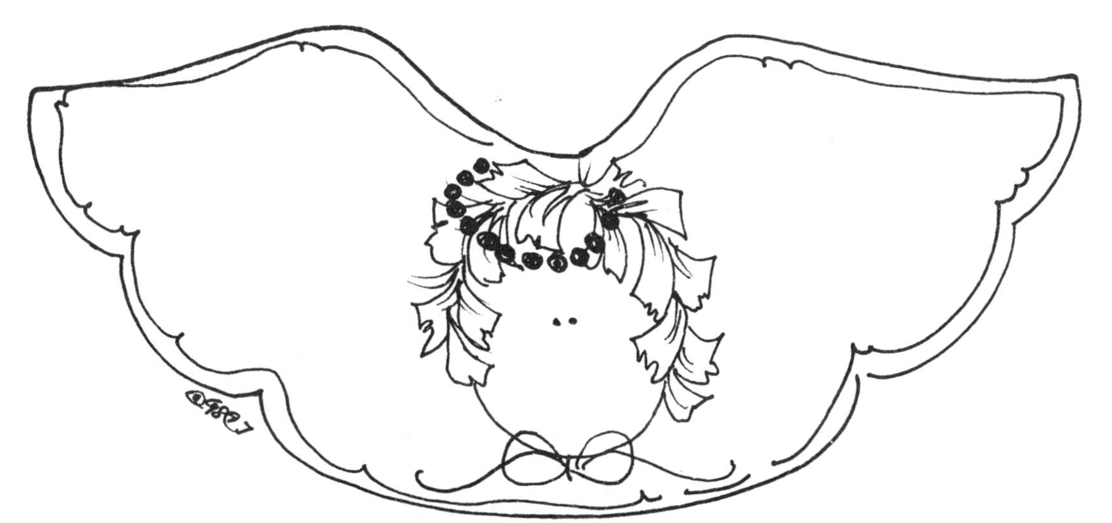

CHRISTMAS STAR MEMORY BOX

DecoArt Americana Colors:

DA1 White
DA112 Cranberry Wine
DA107 Teal Green
DA184 French Vanilla
DA158 Antique Teal
DA43 Salem Blue
DA26 Mauve
DA65 Dk. Chocolate
DA67 Black

DecoArt Royal Metallics:

DM03 Royal Gold

DecoArt Patio Paints:

DCP18 Woodland Brown

DecoArt Specialty Product:

DAS13 Matte Spray

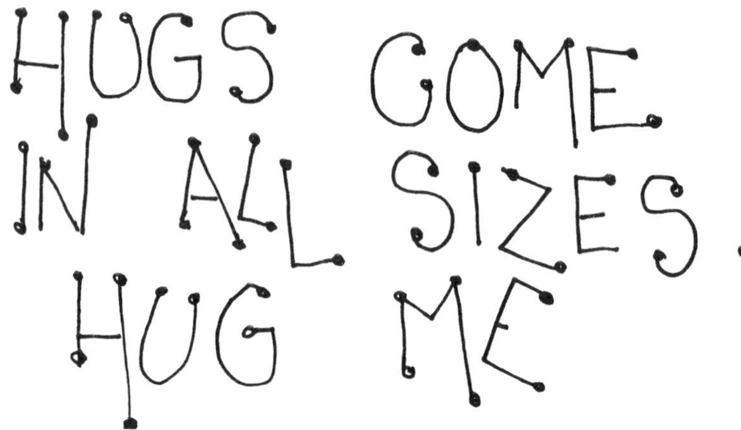

Surfaces by DC&C

Star Memory Box #28-4287

Painting Instructions:

1. Basecoat the bottom of the box in **French Vanilla**, lid **Antique Teal** and star frame on top and stars on sides in **Royal Gold**.
2. Dot the lid with **Salem Blue.**
3. Do the branches in **Dk. Chocolate.**
4. Basecoat the leaves in **Teal Green.** Dot with **Salem Blue.** Float the shadows with **Antique Teal** and the highlights with **Salem Blue.**
5. Basecoat the berries with **Mauve.** Float the shadows with **Cranberry Wine** and dot the highlights with **White.**
6. Spray with **Matte Spray.** Antique all areas except the stars and frame with **Woodland Brown.**

CHRISTMAS STAR MEMORY BOX

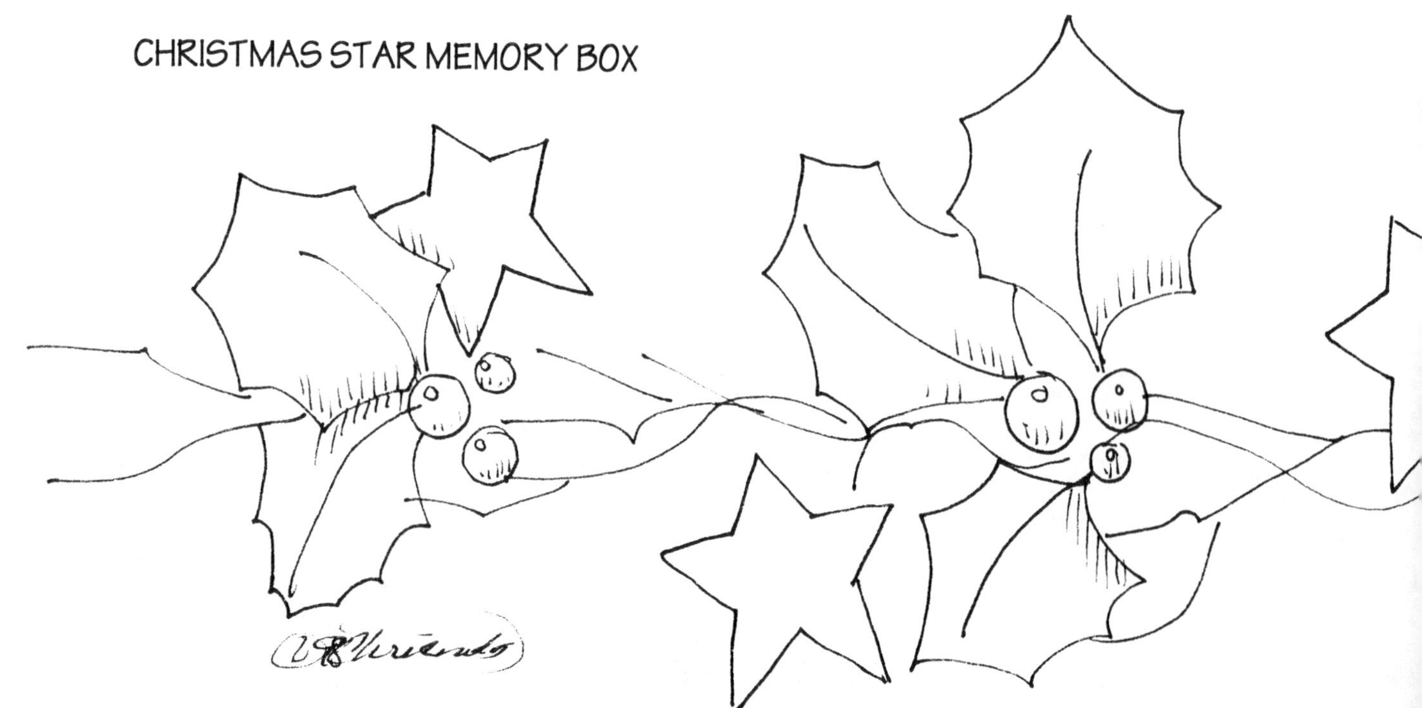

CHRISTMAS TREE STACK BOXES

DecoArt Americana Colors:

DA1 White
DA133 Hauser Dark Green
DA65 Dk. Chocolate
DA86 Uniform Blue
DA43 Salem Blue
DA7 Moon Yellow
DA62 Terra-cotta
DA160 Antique Maroon
DA67 Black
DA60 Mocha
DA18 Country Red
DA58 Antique White
DA49 Dark Pine
DA3 Buttermilk

DecoArt Patio Paints:

DCP18 Woodland Brown

DecoArt Specialty Product:

DAS9 Snow Tex
DAS13 Matte Spray
DS17 Multi Purpose Sealer

DecoArt Royal Metallics:

DM01 Pale Gold

Surfaces by DC&C

Stack Tree Boxes #28-0018
Tin-tiques:
Snowman #24-7136 , Three Stars #24-7223

Miscellaneous Supplies:

Hot Glue Gun
Buttons
Tacky Glue
Palette Knife

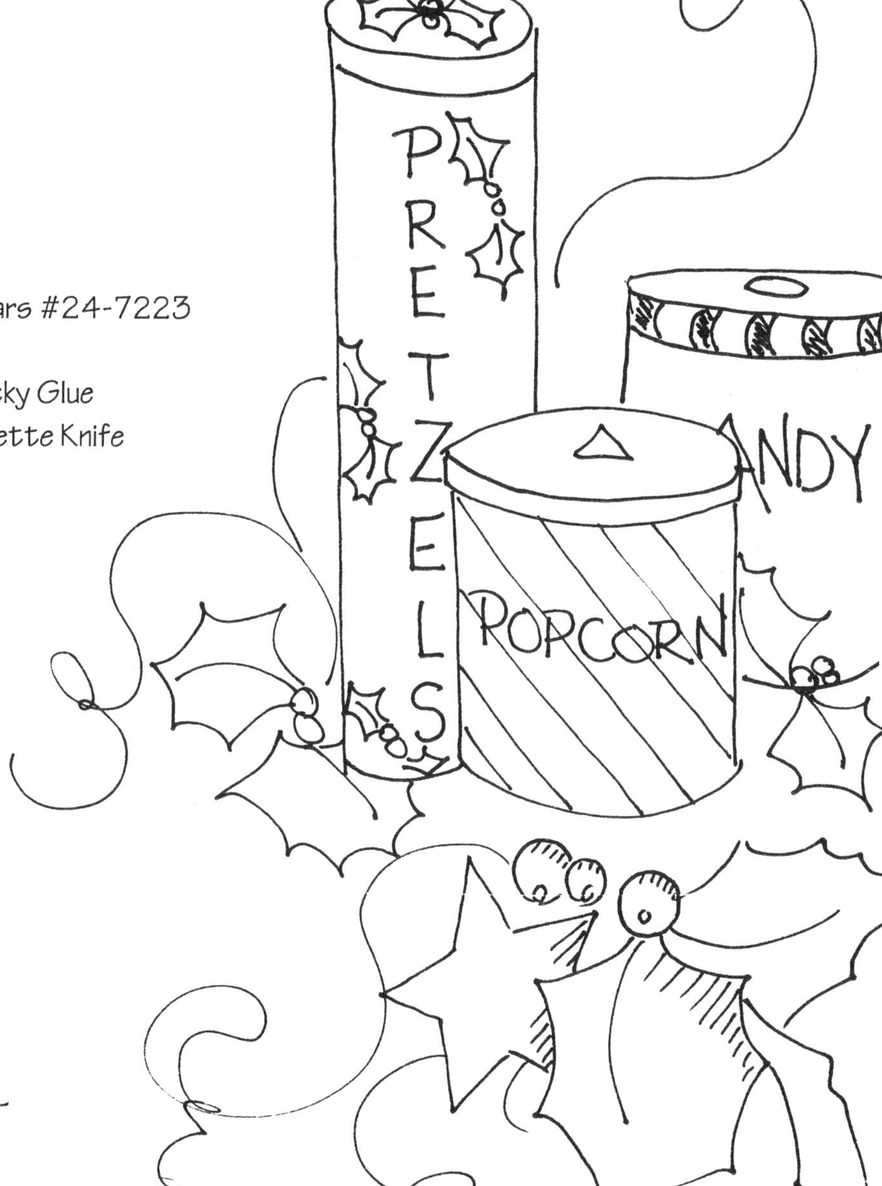

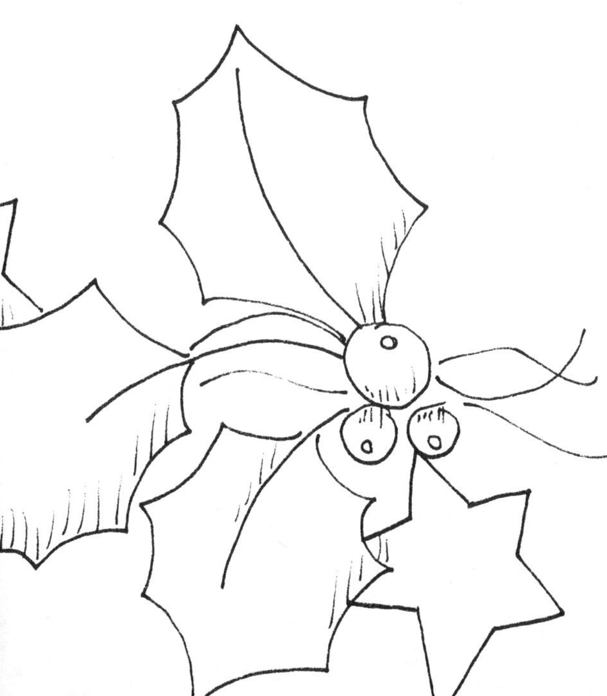

CHRISTMAS TREE STACKING BOXES

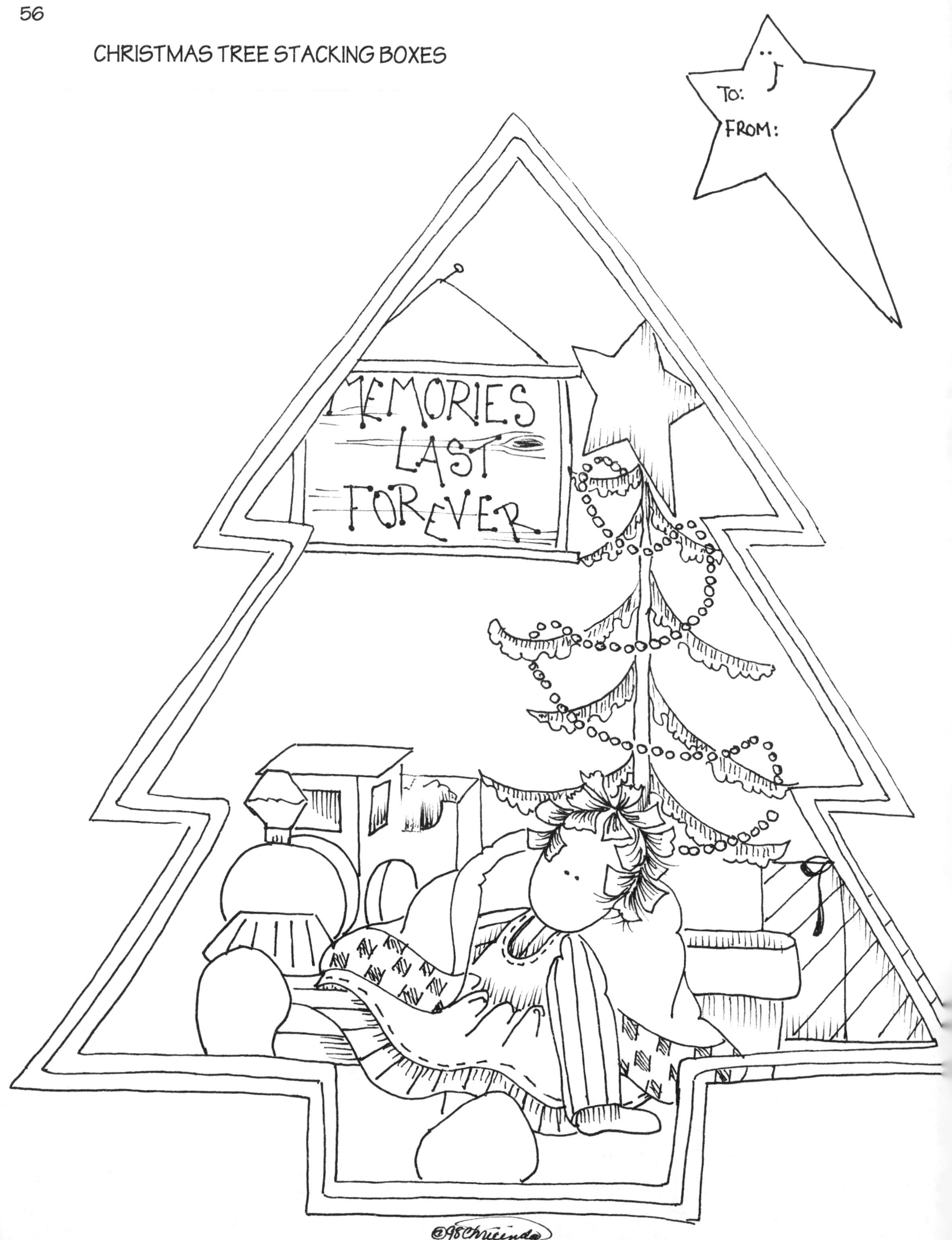

Continued CHRISTMAS TREE STACKING BOXES

Painting Instructions:

1. On all boxes and lids (except for the middle lid where pattern goes) with a palette knife apply **Snow Tex** heavily.
2. Basecoat all of these areas in **Dk. Pine.** Dry-brush with **Salem Blue** and then with **Pale Gold.** Glue buttons and Tin-Tiques in place on large box. Antique with **Woodland Brown.** Dry-brush again in splotchy areas with **Pale Gold.**

Christmas Scene on Middle Lid:

1. Basecoat in **Buttermilk.**
2. Basecoat the package, parts of train and stockings in **Country Red.** Stripe the package with **Moon Yellow.** Float the shadows with **Antique Maroon,** and the highlights with **White** plus a touch of **Terra-cotta.**

Christmas Scene on Middle Lid: continued

3. Basecoat the pot in **Terra-cotta,** float the shadows with **Antique Maroon** and the highlights with **White** plus a touch of **Terre-cotta.**
4. Basecoat the tree trunk in **Dk. Chocolate.** Stipple the greenery with **HauserDark Green** tipped in **White.** Dot with **Country Red.**
5. Basecoat the star and the yellow parts of the train in **Moon Yellow,** float the shadows with **Terra-cotta** and the highlights with **White.**
6. Basecoat her dress and the blue parts of the train in **Uniform Blue.** Stripe her dress with **Terra-cotta.** Float the highlights with **White** plus a touch of **Uniform Blue.**
7. Basecoat her apron and the sign in **Antique White.** Float the shadows with **Dk. Chocolate** and the highlights with **White.** Frame the plaque with **Dk. Chocolate.**
8. Basecoat the blanket in **White.** Check with **Hauser Dark Green** and stripe with **Country Red.** Float the shadows with **Uniform Blue** and the highlights with **White** plus a touch of **Moon Yellow.**
9. Basecoat the flesh areas in **Mocha.** Float the shadows lightly with **Dk. Chocolate,** and the pink areas with **White** plus a touch of **Country Red.**
10. Do her hair in **Terra-cotta.**
11. Do the band around the lid in **Pale Gold.**
12. Do all liner-work with **Black.**
13. Spray with **Matte Spray** and antique with **Woodland Brown.**

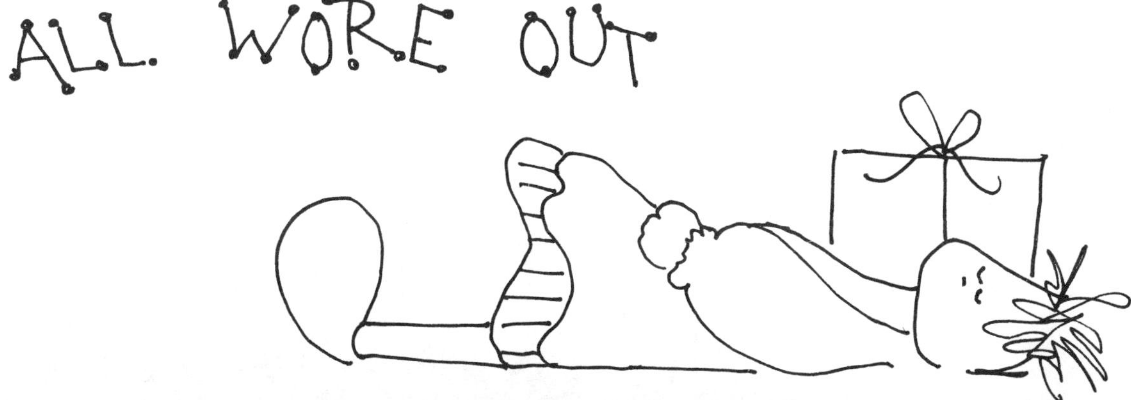

CHRISTMAS NATIVITY ANGEL, GOURD, CANDLE PACKAGE

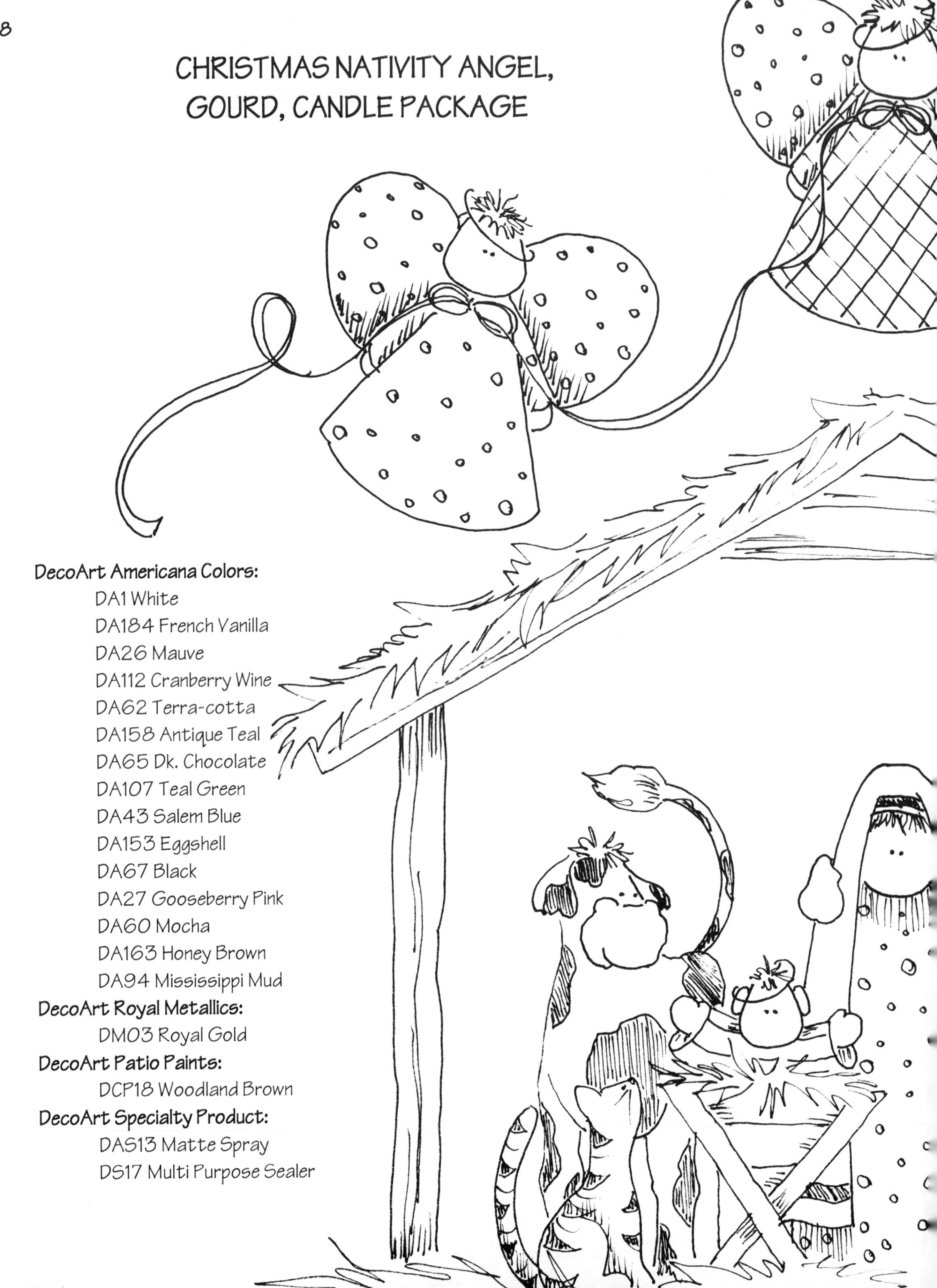

DecoArt Americana Colors:

DA1 White
DA184 French Vanilla
DA26 Mauve
DA112 Cranberry Wine
DA62 Terra-cotta
DA158 Antique Teal
DA65 Dk. Chocolate
DA107 Teal Green
DA43 Salem Blue
DA153 Eggshell
DA67 Black
DA27 Gooseberry Pink
DA60 Mocha
DA163 Honey Brown
DA94 Mississippi Mud

DecoArt Royal Metallics:

DM03 Royal Gold

DecoArt Patio Paints:

DCP18 Woodland Brown

DecoArt Specialty Product:

DAS13 Matte Spray
DS17 Multi Purpose Sealer

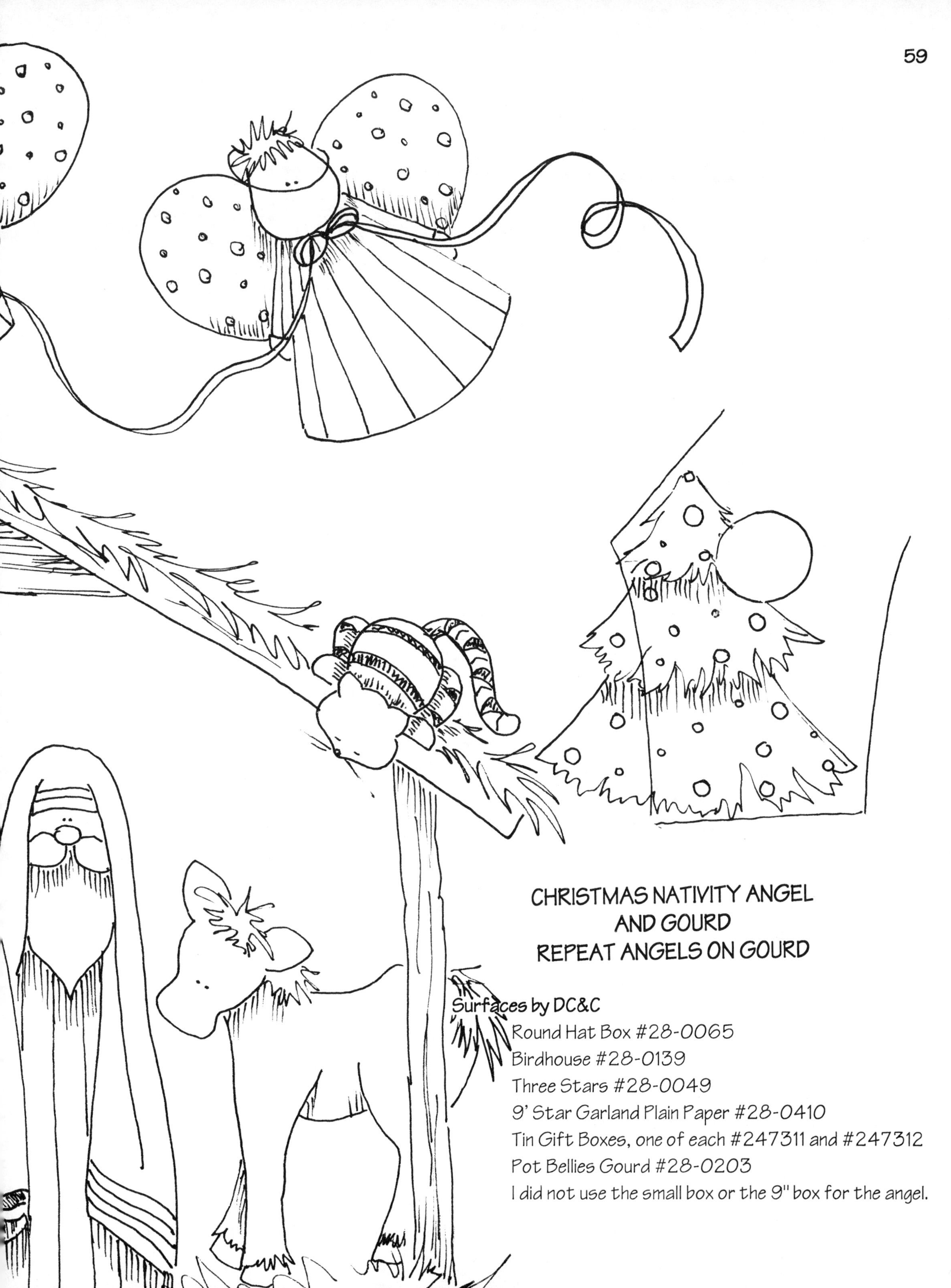

CHRISTMAS NATIVITY ANGEL
AND GOURD
REPEAT ANGELS ON GOURD

Surfaces by DC&C

Round Hat Box #28-0065
Birdhouse #28-0139
Three Stars #28-0049
9' Star Garland Plain Paper #28-0410
Tin Gift Boxes, one of each #247311 and #247312
Pot Bellies Gourd #28-0203
I did not use the small box or the 9" box for the angel.

Continued CHRISTMAS NATIVITY ANGEL, GOURD, CANDLE PACKAGE

Miscellaneous Supplies:

Seawool Sponge
8"x20" stripe for bow
One Ornamental Scroll
Hot Glue Gun
Spanish Moss
Bunches of unbleached muslin fabric knotted for hair
Fabric for wings 2 pieces
Six Mushroom Birds

Painting Instructions:

1. Basecoat the two bottom boxes, large lid and gourd in **French Vanilla**. Basecoat the top box in **Mocha**. Basecoat the collar lid in **Antique Teal**. With seawool sponge apply **Royal Gold** to the halo lid, large stars and star garland. Dry-brush with **Royal Gold** the bow and candle cups on packages.
2. Basecoat the cow in **White** plus a touch of **Eggshell**. Do spots in **Black**. Float the shadows with **Eggshell** plus a touch of **Black**, float highlights with **White**.
3. Basecoat the angels wings in **Eggshell**, float the shadows with **Eggshell** plus a touch of **Lt. Cinnamon**. Do dots and float highlights with **White**.
4. Basecoat all of the flesh areas in **Mocha**, float the shadows with **Lt. Cinnamon** and do the cheeks with **Gooseberry Pink**. Basecoat all of the hair except Jesus's in **Dk. Chocolate**, float the shadows with **Black** and the highlights with **White** plus a touch of **Dk. Chocolate**.
5. Basecoat Joseph's robe and one angel dress in **Teal Green**, do stripes or dots in **Salem Blue**. Float the shadows with **Antique Teal**. Basecoat his hood in **White** plus a touch of **Teal Green**. Stripe with **White**. Float the shadows with **Antique Teal**, float the highlights with **White**.
6. Basecoat Mary's robe and one angel dress in **Mauve**. Do the stripes and dots with **White** plus a touch of **Mauve**. Float the shadows with **Cranberry Wine**. Basecoat Mary's hood in **White** plus a touch of **Mauve**. Do stripes with **Antique Teal** and **White**. Float the shadows with **Cranberry Wine** and the highlights with **White**.
7. Basecoat Jesus's robe and one angel dress in **Eggshell** plus a touch of **Ultra Blue Deep**, add a little more blue and do stripes and float shadows. Do his hair in **Honey Brown**.
8. Basecoat the peak of the roof, cradle and the donkey in **Mississippi Mud**. Float the shadows with **Dk. Chocolate** and the highlights with **White** plus a touch of **Mississippi Mud**. Basecoat the donkey's hair and the poles and roof in **Dk. Chocolate**, float the shadows with **Black** and the highlights with **Mississippi Mud** plus a touch of **White**.
9. Basecoat the hay in **Honey Brown**. Float the shadows with **Dk. Chocolate** and streak the highlights with **White** plus a touch of **Honey Brown**.
10. Basecoat the cats in **Terra-cotta**, do stripes with **Dk. Chocolate** and **French Vanilla**. Float the shadows with **Dk. Chocolate** and highlights with **French Vanilla**.

Birdhouse:

1. Basecoat the walls in **Mauve** and the roof in **Honey Brown**.
2. Basecoat the tree in **Antique Teal**. Stroke the highlights with **White** plus a touch of **Antique Teal**. Dot with **French Vanilla, Cranberry Wine** plus a touch of **Mauve** and **Salem Blue.**

To Finish all Pieces:

1. Do all liner-work with **Black**.
2. Spray with **Matte Spray** and antique all pieces with **Woodland Brown**.
3. Cut the wings, stitch leaving a small opening, stuff with poly-fill and finsih stitching. Tear hair into 1"x6" pieces of muslin tie a knot in the middle and glue in place. It takes a bunch! Assemble the rest according to color picture.

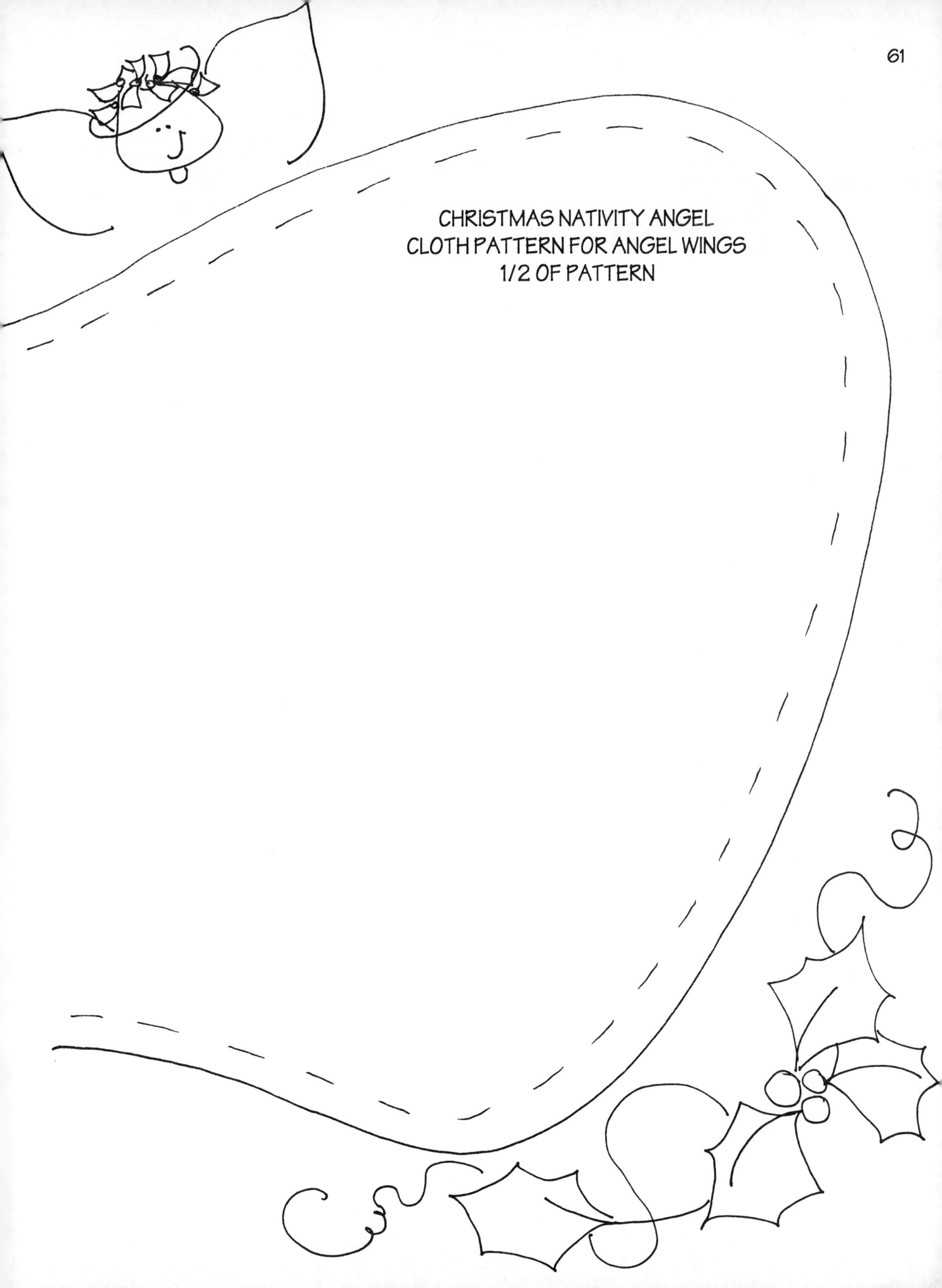
CHRISTMAS NATIVITY ANGEL
CLOTH PATTERN FOR ANGEL WINGS
1/2 OF PATTERN

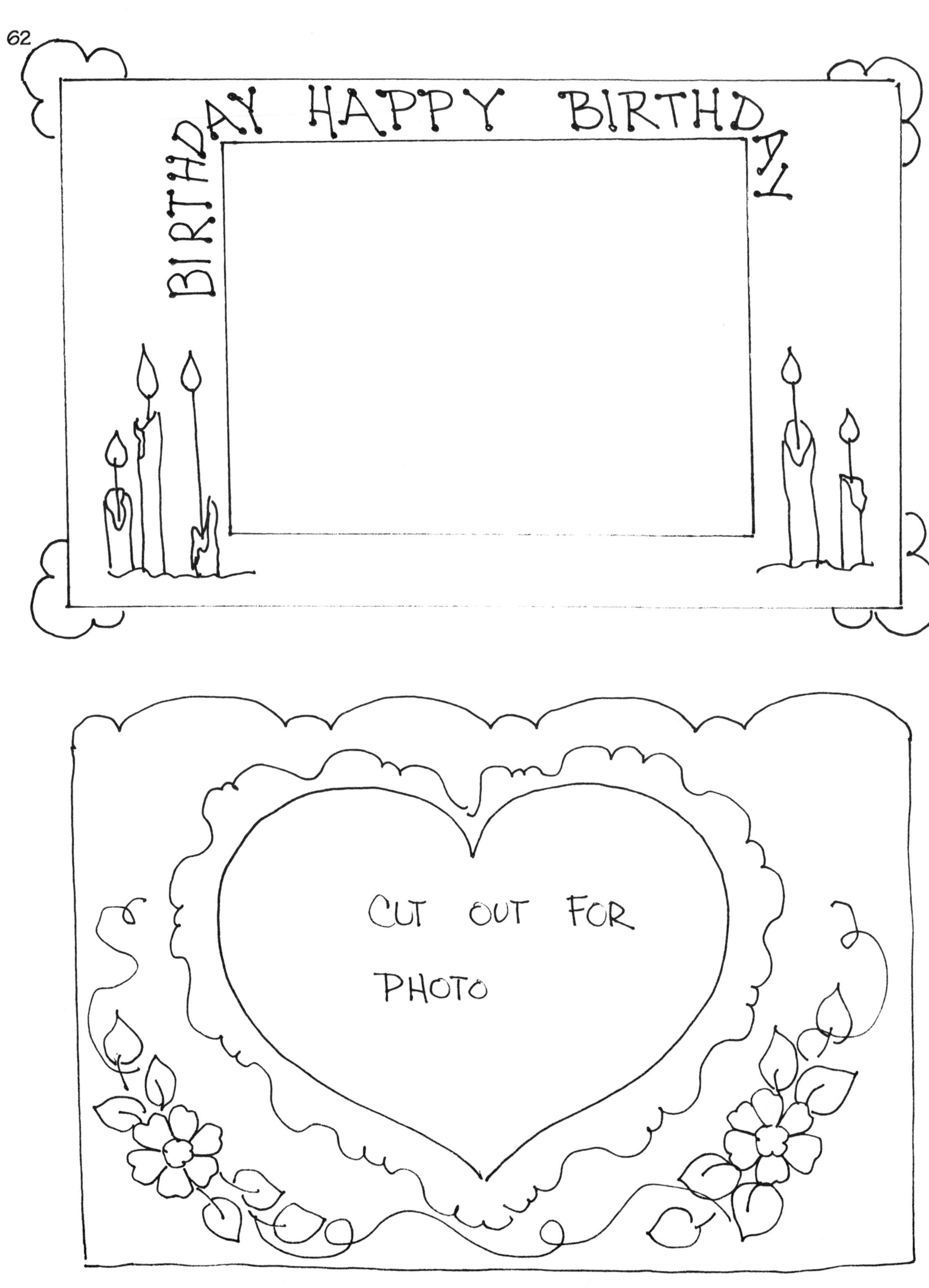
HAPPY BIRTHDAY
BIRTHDAY
BIRTHDAY
CUT OUT FOR
PHOTO

Susan Scheewe Publications, Inc.

13435 N.E. Whitaker Way Portland, Or. 97230 PH (503) 254-9100 FAX (503) 252-9508

ACRYLIC BOOKS

Vol.	Title	No.	Price
Vol. 19	"Gift of Painting" by Susan Scheewe	230	$9.50
Vol. 1	"Painting It's Our Bag" by Bev Hink/Susan Scheewe	193	$9.50
Vol. 4	"Keepsake Sampler" by Susan & Camille Scheewe	200	$9.50
Vol. 1	"Keepsakes For The Holidays" by C. Stempel & S. Scheewe	286	$9.50
Vol. 1	"Bumbleberries" by Connie Aloise *NEW	412	$9.50
Vol. 2	'Country Heartworks 2" by Reed Baxter	365	$9.50
Vol. 3	"Country Heartworks 3" by Reed Baxter	402	$9.50
Vol. 1	"Plain Folk" by Ginger Barlage	389	$9.50
Vol. 1	"Kids And Water" by Joyce Benner	234	$9.50
Vol. 2	"The Flower Market" by Joyce Benner	319	$9.50
Vol. 3	"Country Fixin's - For All Seasons" by Rhonda Caldwell	332	$9.50
Vol. 1	"Country Celebration" by Tammy Christensen	378	$9.50
Vol. 1	"A Painters Garden" by Jane Dillon	354	$9.50
Vol. 2	"A Painter's Garden 2" by Jane Dillon *NEW	411	$9.50
Vol. 1	"Santas and Sams" by Bobi Dolara	258	$9.50
Vol. 2	"Vintage Peace" by Bobi Dolara	270	$9.50
Vol. 2	"Floral Designs 2" by Carol Empet	338	$9.50
Vol. 3	"Floral Portraits" by Carol Empet	358	$9.50
Vol. 1	"Angels Are Near" by Carol Freeman & Brenda Turley	375	$9.50
Vol. 1	"Briar Patch" by Sandy Fochler	380	$9.50
Vol. 2	"Briar Patch #2" by Sandy Fochler *NEW	424	$9.50
Vol. 1	"Romantically Tole Bauernmalerei" by Sherry Gall	311	$9.50
Vol. 2	"Deck The Halls Bauernmalerei" by Sherry Gall	391	$9.50
Vol. 1	"Olde Thyme Folk Art" by Teresa Gregory	390	$9.50
Vol. 2	"Country Thyme" by Teresa Gregory	406	$9.50
Vol. 1	'Windchimes, Weathervanes & Welcomes" by Vickie Higley	386	$9.50
Vol. 1	"Holiday Gathering" by Angie Hupp	267	$9.50
Vol. 3	"Heavenly Gathering" by Angie Hupp	320	$9.50
Vol. 1	"Happy Heart, Happy Home" by Cathy Jones	241	$9.50
Vol. 1	"Dandelions" by Carla Kern *NEW	416	$9.50
Vol. 1	"Pickets & Pastimes" by Marie & Jim King	329	$9.50
Vol. 3	"Pickets & Pastimes 3, Feathered Inns" by M. & J. King	385	$9.50
Vol. 1	"For Me & My House" by Myrna King	370	$9.50
Vol. 1	"Huckleberry Horse" by Hanna Long	269	$9.50
Vol. 2	"Love Lives Here" by Mary Lynn Lewis	185	$6.50
Vol. 3	"Love Lives Here" by Mary Lynn Lewis	195	$6.50
Vol. 1	"Everything Under The Moon" by Jackie Ludwig *NEW	421	$9.50
Vol. 1	"Second Nature" by Kathy McPherson *NEW	427	$9.50
Vol. 2	"Special Welcomes" by Corinne Miller	298	$9.50
Vol. 3	"Special Welcomes #3, Crazy About Crafting" by Corinne Miller	309	$9.50
Vol. 5	"Special Welcomes #5 All Wrapped Up" by Corinne Miller	333	$9.50
Vol. 6	"Special Welcomes #6 Crop Keepers" by Corinne Miller	347	$9.50
Vol. 1	"Fruit & Flower Fantasies" by Joyce Morrison	277	$9.50
Vol. 2	"Fruit & Flower Fantasies 2" by Joyce Morrison	382	$9.50
Vol. 1	"Whimsical Critters" by Lori Ohlson	228	$7.50
Vol. 2	"Sunflower Farm" by Lori Ohlson	326	$9.50
Vol. 1	"Friends Forevermore" by Karen Ortman *NEW	434	$9.50
Vol. 1	"Holiday Medley" by Nina Owens	265	$9.50
Vol. 2	"Another Holiday Medley" by Nina Owens	296	$9.50
Vol. 1	"Oh Those Little Rascals" by Diane Permenter	247	$9.50
Vol. 1	"Tailfeathers" by Gisele Pope & Carla Kern *NEW	417	$9.50
Vol. 8	"Now & Then" by La Rae Parry *NEW	428	$9.50
Vol. 1	"Between The Vines" by Jamie Mills Price	400	$9.50
Vol. 2	"Between The Vines 2" by Jamie Mills Price *NEW	419	$9.50
Vol. 1	"Forever In My Heart" by Diane Richards.....AC/Fabric	188	$6.50
Vol. 2	"Memories In My Heart" by Diane Richards.....AC/Fabric	189	$6.50
Vol. 3	"Forever In My Heart II" by Diane Richards.....AC/Fabric	205	$9.50
Vol. 6	"Angels In My Stocking" by Diane Richards	254	$9.50
Vol. 7	"Nostalgic Dreams" by Diane Richards	273	$9.50
Vol. 8	"Angel Kisses" by Diane Richards	346	$9.50
Vol. 1	"Country Classics" by Karen Rideout *NEW	413	$9.50
Vol. 1	"Country Fun For Chistmas" by Tina Rodrigues	367	$9.50
Vol. 2	"Country Fun 2" by Tina Rodrigues	383	$9.50
Vol. 3	"Country At Heart" by Tina Rodrigues	401	$9.50
Vol. 4	"Country At Heart 4" by Tina Rodrigues	410	$9.50
Vol. 1	"Kracker Jack Kritters" by Kathie Rueger	405	$9.50
Vol. 1	"Schoolhouse Treasures" by Cathy Schmidt	408	$9.50
Vol. 2	"Schoolhouse Treasures" by Cathy Schmidt *NEW	433	$9.50
Vol. 1	"Holiday Hangarounds" by Marsha Sellers	327	$9.50
Vol. 1	"Huckleberry Friends" by Cheryl Seslar	393	$9.50
Vol. 2	"Huckleberry Friends 2" by Cheryl Seslar	403	$9.50
Vol. 3	"Huckleberry Friends 3" by Cheryl Seslar *NEW	431	$9.50
Vol. 1	"Creations In Canvas...and More" by Carol Spooner	256	$9.50
Vol. 1	"Gran's Garden" by Ros Stallcup	295	$9.50
Vol. 2	"Another Gran's Garden" by Ros Stallcup	315	$9.50
Vol. 3	"Gran's Garden & House" by Ros Stallcup	334	$9.50
Vol. 4	"Gran's Garden Party" by Ros Stallcup	345	$9.50
Vol. 5	"Gran's Treasures" by Ros Stallcup	363	$9.50
Vol. 6	"Gran's Gifts" by Ros Stallcup	387	$9.50
Vol. 7	"Gran's Welcome" by Ros Stallcup *NEW	425	$9.50
Vol. 8	"Gran's Marketplace" by Ros Stallcup *NEW	426	$12.95
Vol. 1	"Blackberry Hollow" by Margaret Steed	384	$9.50
Vol. 2	"Blackberry Hollow" by Margaret Steed	407	$9.50
Vol. 1	"Mrs. McGregors Garden" by Charleen Stempel	316	$9.50
Vol. 1	"Christmas Greetings from the Cottage" by Chris Stokes	336	$9.50
Vol. 1	"Christmas Visions" by Max Terry	278	$9.50
Vol. 3	"Painting Clay Pot-pourri" by Max Terry	310	$9.50
Vol. 4	"The Nesting Place" by Max Terry	373	$9.50
Vol. 1	"Country Primitives" by Maxine Thomas	274	$9.50
Vol. 2	"Country Primitives 2" by Maxine Thomas	300	$9.50
Vol. 3	"Country Primitives 3" by Maxine Thomas	322	$9.50
Vol. 4	"Country Primitives 4" by Maxine Thomas	350	$9.50
Vol. 5	"Country Primitives 5" by Maxine Thomas	392	$9.50
Vol. 6	"Country Primitives 6" by Maxine Thomas *NEW	429	$9.50
Vol. 1	"Rise & Shine" by Jolene Thompson	214	$6.50
Vol. 2	"Garden Gate" by Jolene Thompson	250	$9.50
Vol. 5	"Count Your Blessings" by Chris Thornton	213	$9.50
Vol. 6	"Share Your Blessings" by Chris Thornton	226	$9.50
Vol. 7	"Blessings" by Chris Thornton	255	$9.50
Vol. 9	"Blessings For The Home" by Chris Thornton	275	$9.50
Vol. 11	"Painted Blessings" by Chris Thornton	323	$9.50
Vol. 12	"Family Blessings" by Chris Thornton	349	$9.50
Vol. 13	"Garden Blessings" by Chris Thornton	356	$9.50
Vol. 14	"Friendship Blessings" by Chris Thorton	371	$9.50
Vol. 15	"Multitude of Blessings" by Chris Thorton	379	$9.50
Vol. 16	"10th Aniversary of Blessings" by Chris Thornton *NEW	404	$9.50
Vol. 17	"Blessings For The Home & Garden" by Chris Thornton	423	$12.95
Vol. 1	"Watermelon Wedges and Rustic Edges" by Lorinne Thurlow	342	$9.50
Vol. 3	"Watermelon Wedges and Rustic Edges 3" by L. Thurlow	362	$9.50
Vol. 2	"Farmer and Friends" by Lou Ann Trice	366	$9.50
Vol. 5	"Daydreams & Sweet Shirts II" by Don & Lynn Weed	208	$9.50
Vol. 1	"Pitter-Patter-Pigtail-Girls! A Simpler Thyme" by Stacy Gross West *NEW	432	$9.50
Vol. 1	"Connie's Favorite Old-Time Labels" by Connie Williams	335	$9.50
Vol. 2	"Connie's Garden Seed Packets" by Connie Williams	351	$9.50
Vol. 1	"Floral Fabrics and Watercolor" by Sally Williams	262	$9.50
Vol. 1	"A Time For Giving" by Evelyn Wright	308	$9.50
Vol. 1	"Heart Full Of Whimsy" by Mariellen Youngdahl *NEW	420	$9.50

7-20-98

NAME ______________________

ADDRESS ______________________

____

CITY/STATE/ZIP ______________________

____

PH ( ) ______________________

VISA ______________________

M/C ______________________

EXP. DATE ______________________

SHIPPING $ ______________________

SHIP TO: ______________________

****

SHIPPING & HANDLING CHARGES

Add $3.00 for the First Book for shipping and handling. Add $1.50 per each additional book.

Please Add $4.00 for handling & postage. PER TAPES. Sorry we must have a "NO REFUND - NO RETURN" policy.

U.S CURRENCY

LOOK FOR US ON-LINE!
http://www.painting-books.com
e-mail us: SCHEEWEPUB@aol.com

VISA MasterCard

PRICES SUBJECT TO CHANGE WITHOUT NOTICE

FOR MORE INFORMATION ON BOOKS OR SUPPLIES CALL OR WRITE US

WE ARE ALWAYS GLAD TO HEAR FROM YOU!

Susan Scheewe Publications Inc.

13435 N.E. Whitaker Way Portland, Or. 97230 PH (503) 254-9100 FAX (503) 252-9508

WATERCOLOR BOOKS

	Vol. 20	"Simply Country Watercolors" by Susan Scheewe Brown	257	$9.50 ___
	Vol. 21	"Simply Watercolor" by Susan Scheewe Brown.....T.V. Book	260	$11.95 ___
	Vol. 24	"Introduction to Watercolor" by Susan Scheewe Brown.....T.V. Book	314	$11.95 ___
	Vol. 25	"Watercolors Anyone Can Paint" by Susan Scheewe Brown...T.V. Book	325	$11.95 ___
	Vol. 26	"Watercolor - The Garden Scene" by Susan Scheewe Brown... T.V. Book	339	$11.95 ___
	Vol. 27	"Watercolor Landscapes" by Susan Scheewe Brown....T.V. Book	360	$11.95 ___
	Vol. 28	"Watercolor - Garden Treasures" by Susan Scheewe Brown....T.V. Book	361	$11.95 ___
	Vol. 29	"Watercolor Collection" by Susan Scheewe Brown....T.V. Book	374	$11.95 ___
*NEW	Vol. 30	"Scheewe Art Workshop - Watercolor & Acrylic" by Susan Scheewe Brown..T.V. Bk.	398	$11.95 ___
*NEW	Vol. 31	"Enjoy Watercolor & Acrylic" by Susan Scheewe Brown.....T.V. Book	399	$11.95 ___
*NEW	Vol. 32	"Le Jardin" by Susan Scheewe Brown.....T.V. Book	414	$12.95 ___
*NEW	Vol. 33	"Simply Acrylic & Watercolor" by Susan Scheewe Brown.....T.V. Book	418	$12.95 ___
	Vol. 7	"Watercolor Journey" by Ellie Cook	381	$9.50 ___
	Vol. 3	"Watercolor Made Easy 3" by Kathy George	301	$9.50 ___
*NEW	Vol. 1	"Watercolor for Real" by Robert and Sharon Long	409	$9.50 ___
	Vol. 1	"The Way I Started" by Gary Hawk	120	$6.00 ___
	Vol. 1	"Watercolor Fun & Easy" by Beverly Kaiser	243	$7.50 ___
	Vol. 7	"Watercolor Charms" by Sharon Rachal	376	$9.50 ___

LOOK FOR US ON-LINE!
e-mail us: SCHEEWEPUB@aol.com

NAME ______________________

____

ADDRESS ______________________

____

CITY/STATE/ZIP ______________________

____

PH( ) ______________________

VISA ______________________

M/C ______________________

EXP. DATE ______________________

SHIPPING $ ______________________

SHIP TO ______________________

____

____

7-20
-98

VIDEOS BY SUSAN SCHEEWE BROWN

"Scheewe Art Workshop I" 13-1/2 HR Shows On 4 Tapes/ Introduction to Watercolors	S8225	$69.99
"Scheewe Art Workshop II" 13-1/2 HR Shows On 4 Tapes/ Watercolors Anyone Can Paint	S8223	$69.99
"Scheewe Art Workshop III" 13 - 1/2 HR Shows On 4 Tapes/ The Garden Scene	S8375	$69.99
"Scheewe Art Workshop III B" 13 - 1/2 HR Shows On 4 Tapes/ Watercolor Landscapes	S8376	$69.99
"Watercolor Painting with Children" 1 Hour	S8222	$19.99 ___
"Fabric Painting Fun" 1 Hour		$24.99 ___
"Watercolor Techniques" 1 Hour	S8226	$19.99 ___
"Painting Projects" Watercolor 3 Hours...Trees and Leaves	S8224	$49.99 ___
"Acrylic Techniques For Everyone" I Hour	S8368	$19.99 ___

PEN & INK BOOKS / COLORED PENCIL BOOKS

Vol. 6	"Journey of Memories" by Claudia Nice	166	$6.50 ___
Vol. 7	"Scenes from Seasons Past" by Claudia Nice	183	$9.50 ___
Vol. 8	"Taste of Summer" by Claudia Nice	223	$9.50 ___
Vol. 2	"Colored Pencil Made Easy" by Jane Wunder	242	$7.50 ___
Vol. 3	"The Beauty of Colored Pencil and Ink Drawing" by Jane Wunder	259	$7.50 ___
Vol. 4	"Watercolor, Pen and Ink" by Jane Wunder	357	$9.50 ___
Vol. 5	"Watercolor, Pen and Ink, Vol. 2" by Jane Wunder *NEW	422	$9.50 ___

OILS BOOKS

Vol. 1	"His and Hers" by Susan Scheewe	101	$6.50 ___
Vol. 7	"Paint 'n Patch" by Susan Scheewe	107	$5.50 ___
Vol. 11	"I Love To Paint" by Susan Scheewe	111	$6.50 ___
Vol. 14	"Enjoy Painting Animals" by Susan Scheewe	114	$6.50 ___
Vol. 19	"Gift Of Painting" by Susan Scheewe O/AC/WC	230	$9.50 ___
Vol. 1	"Western Images" by Becky Anthony	186	$6.50 ___
Vol. 5	"Soft Petals" by Georgia Bartlett	171	$6.50 ___
Vol. 6	"Painting Fantasy Flowers" by Georgia Bartlett	215	$7.50 ___
Vol. 8	"Petals" by Georgia Bartlett	317	$9.50 ___
Vol. 9	"Floral Medley" by Georgia Bartlett	344	$9.50 ___
Vol. 10	"Flower Show" by Georgia Bartlett *NEW	415	$9.50 ___
Vol. 4	"Countryscapes" by Donna Bell	249	$9.50 ___
Vol. 5	"Painter to Painter" by Donna Bell	263	$9.50 ___
Vol. 6	"Landscapes With Acrylics & Oil" by Donna Bell	282	$9.50 ___
Vol. 1	"Natures Palette" by Carol Binford.....O/AC	248	$9.50 ___
Vol. 2	"Oil Painting The Easy Way" by Bill Blackman	337	$9.50 ___
Vol. 3	"Lighted Windows & Gardens" by Bill Blackman	355	$9.50 ___
Vol. 1	"Mini Mini More" by Terri and Nancy Brown	150	$6.50 ___
Vol. 2	"Mini Mini More" by Terri and Nancy Brown	151	$6.50 ___
Vol. 4	"Heritage Trails" by Terri and Nancy Brown	169	$6.50 ___
Vol. 7	"More Garden Trails" by Terri and Nancy Brown	368	$9.50 ___
Vol. 4	"Windows Of My World 4" by Jackie Claflin	359	$9.50 ___
Vol. 4	"Expressions In Oil" by Delores Egger	239	$7.50 ___
Vol. 2	"Days of Heaven" by Gloria Gaffney	252	$9.50 ___
Vol .6	"The Sky's The Limit" by Jean Green	372	$9.50 ___
Vol. 3	"Nature's Beauty" by Bill Huffaker	177	$6.50 ___
Vol. 1	"Ducks and Geese" by Jean Lyles	172	$6.50 ___
Vol. 1	"Raining Cats & Dogs" by Todd Mallett	304	$9.50 ___
Vol. 2	"Another Path To Follow" by Lee McGowen	328	$9.50 ___
Vol. 1	"Bitterroot Backroads" by Glenice Moore-Nickel	330	$9.50 ___
Vol. 2	"Bitterroot Backroads 2" by Glenice Moore-Nickel	340	$9.50 ___
Vol. 3	"Bitterroot Backroads 3" by Glenice Moore-Nickel	369	$9.50 ___
Vol. 1	"Stepping Stones" by Judy Nutter	121	$6.50 ___
Vol. 1	"Painting with Paulson" by Buck Paulson	343	$11.95 ___
Vol. 1	"Rustic Charms" by Sharon Rachal	175	$6.50 ___
Vol. 2	"Rustic Charms II" by Sharon Rachal	199	$9.50 ___
Vol. 5	"Rustic Charms V, Florals" by Sharon Rachal	261	$9.50 ___
Vol. 1	"Painting Flowers With Augie" by Augie Reis	152	$6.50 ___
Vol. 3	"Realistic Technique" by Judy Sleight	341	$9.50 ___
Vol. 2	"Soft & Misty Paintings" by Kathy Snider	229	$9.50 ___
Vol. 4	"Friends We've Known" by Gene Waggoner	187	$7.50 ___
Vol. 5	"Friends Are Forever" by Gene Waggoner	231	$7.50 ___
Vol. 1	"Fantasy Folk" by Don Weed	123	$6.50 ___
Vol. 1	"Something Special For Everyone" by Mildred Yeiser	158	$6.50 ___
Vol. 5	"Soft & Gentle Paintings" by Mildred Yeiser	268	$9.50 ___

SHIPPING & HANDLING CHARGES
Add $3.00 for the First Book for shipping and handling.
Add $1.50 per each additional book.
Please Add $4.00 for handling & postage. PER TAPES. Sorry we must have a "NO REFUND - NO RETURN" policy.
U.S CURRENCY